Lives in Cricket: number

LCH Palairet
Stylist 'Par Excellence'

Darren Senior

First published in Great Britain by
the Association of Cricket Statisticians and Historians Cardiff CF11 9XR
Copyright ACS, 2016

British Library Cataloguing-in-Publication Data.
A catalogue record for this book is available from the British Library.

ISBN: 978 1 908165 72 5
Printed by The City Press Leeds Ltd

Contents

Introduction

It is over a hundred years since Lionel Palairet last played a first class match, yet his name still crops up in the odd cricket book, marking him out to be probably the top batting stylist of his era. My interest in him dates back to the first book I ever bought, Roy Webber's *County Cricket Championship* published in 1957. It was here that I first made a connection with him. I bought Benny Green's *Wisden Cricket Anthology 1864-1900* in 1979; this included a number of scorecards in which he appeared. As a result of reading this book, I joined the ACS as a teenager and my interest in Lionel Palairet steadily grew.

It has taken me over 35 years to put pen to paper, although 30 years ago my old friend Robert Brooke said 'write one'. Although noted for the style and grace of his batting, Palairet's achievements and records have gone virtually unreported and largely forgotten. At the time of his death, he still held most of the batting records for Somerset. It was not until the arrival of Harold Gimblett in 1935 that many of the Somerset batting records were beaten; he was unquestionably the best batsman by far Somerset ever had up to Gimblett's arrival.

In addition, he was cricket captain for Oxford University, he also gained a blue at athletics and narrowly missed a football blue. He also played county football for Somerset and Dorset, and enjoyed numerous other sports. He was (like his father) heavily involved in the community he lived in, serving on many committees such as for the Conservative Party and Fisheries Commission, and in golf, and many cricket committees including Devon and Somerset counties.

He led a full life albeit cut a little short; he was a hard-working family man and his contributions to the cricket and the golf world were immense, and whatever his faults as a person, he fully deserves recognition in these fields. My hope is that a look into his career and life leaves readers with an appreciation of his cricket abilities, but also other qualities as an individual and an insight into his family and his background. With this I think you could understand why he was seen by others as a little aloof or distant to other people.

I must thank the ACS committee for giving me the opportunity to share his life, and to Mark Rowe for his encouragement and help in attaining photographs and overall support. I must mention the British Newspaper Archive website, which enabled me access hundreds of newspapers, while sat at my computer working merrily away at home; without this my research would have taken years to complete. Also John Hirst (Devon Golfing Union), Tim Roper, Huw Nathan and Robert Brooke for their proof-reading. In addition, Roger Mann for providing some excellent photographs and also ACS member Roger Moulton, and Graham Skidmore and Ian Tier of the Somerset Stragglers who helped provide some of the scorecards of matches Lionel played in. Many thanks to Kit Bartlett for his careful proof-reading.

Darren R Senior
Brighouse, April 2016

Chapter one
French connections

Lionel Palairet has been dead for over 80 years, yet books are still published today which refer to his graceful batting during the period known by some as 'The Golden Age' of cricket, which is generally considered to be from 1890 to 1914. During his time as a player, he had no equal with regard to the art of batting and the elegant style with which he scored his runs. For Somerset he was truly a great batsman who was full of poise, grace and power. Even at the time of his death he held most of the county's batting records. Outside cricket though, little is known about him. However, researching this book has opened up a lot more about him as a person and about the contributions he made not only to cricket, but to golf, which would take up most of his spare time once he had retired from first class cricket.

He led a full, if not long, life and looking back on his deeds, he could be proud of what he had contributed as a person, as a sportsman and a family man. It is well known that he was from a privileged background; however, as you will read, a lot of tragedy ran through his life. I hope this book shows to readers that he was much more than a great batting stylist, and gives a picture of his life and his deeds that began in the Victorian area and ended well into the 20th century.

It has been stated in several publications that he was of French Huguenot ancestry. A Huguenot is a member of a French Protestant religion which started in the 16th century. Followers were inspired by the 1530's writings of Jean Calvin. Followers mainly lived in the central and southern parts of France. The family line of the Palairets has been traced back to 1475. From the early 1600s, Lionel's family ancestors were living in a town called Montauban, in southern France, 31 miles north of Toulouse. In 1685, King Louis XIV abolished legal recognition of the religion. He then forced all of the Huguenots to convert to the Catholic religion. It is estimated 500,000 fled France. They settled in many countries where they were accepted and allowed to worship freely.

It is estimated that 50,000 of the Huguenots fled to England, many arriving in Kent and eventually moving out into many parts of England. London, Bedfordshire, Norfolk and the South West, which were all popular areas for members to settle. A number of Palairets settled in Holland, initially in Amsterdam or Rotterdam. Another branch went to live in New Zealand.

Going back to Lionel's direct ancestry line, I can start with his great-great grandfather John Gwalter Palairet (1765-1824). He was a barrister at law who married Catherine Pistor in 1795. It is evident that even at this stage, the Palairets were a very upper-class family which they maintained down to Lionel, with the males of the family often being educated to degree level and becoming barristers, high ranking army officers or members of the Church of England in various capacities. In addition marriages were nearly always of a similar social class so children were not allowed to marry beneath themselves; this ensured the class status within the families was maintained.

From this marriage, we have Lionel's grandfather, Septimus Palairet (1807-54). He was to rise to the rank of captain in the 29th Regiment in the British Army. He was born in Wiltshire, though he would actually die in Edinburgh. Septimus would marry twice, firstly to Mary Ann Hamilton (1822-51). She died in Philadelphia, County Durham. In 1853 he would marry Lydia Bedney (1833-87). From these marriages Septimus would have seven children, the second of these being Henry Hamilton (1845-1923), who was Lionel's father.

Henry went to Oxford and played cricket for Exeter College. While at Oxford, he was the eighth rower in the 1865 trial boat race. Unfortunately, he did not make the final Oxford rowing team for that year's race. He also played cricket and was a useful club cricketer. He even played two first class matches for the MCC (1868-69). However, he achieved little of note in these games. It was in archery that he excelled. Henry was six times English Archery champion of England (1876, 1878, and 1880-82); he was also champion of John O'Gaunt's five times (second in importance to the English championship).

For a number of years, he was a Judge at the Court of Assizes in Bath; he was also secretary to the Archery Committee of The All England Club and would organise archery events all over the country. He was also a member of the local Conservative Party and a member of the Somerset County Cricket Club, serving on both committees for many years. Henry would often take the chair at these meetings. Henry's brother General Charles Palairet also served on the Somerset cricket committee for a while during the 1890s.

Up to the age of 30 Henry moved around England fairly regularly, probably due to his work. He lived in Grange-over-Sands for several years until 1873 when he moved to Cattistock Lodge, Cattistock in west Dorset, in the upper reaches of the Frome Valley and eight miles north-west of the county town, Dorchester.

In 1869 Henry married Elizabeth Ann Bigg (1844-79) and the couple had five children: Lionel Charles Hamilton (born 1870), Richard Cameron North (born 1871) and Evelyn Mary (born 1872) at Grange-over-Sands; and Edith Veronica (born 1874) at Cattistock and Rose Eleanor (born 1879) at Holcombe, Devon.

Chapter two
Early life and Repton

Although born in the seaside town of Grange-over-Sands on May 27, 1870, by the time Lionel was four he was living at Cattistock Lodge and he spent his early childhood education at The Reverend Cornish School in Clevedon, as a full time boarder only coming home for holidays. The town of Clevedon is on the north Somerset coast; it is famous for having a pier (opened in 1869). The seafront has ornamental gardens, a Victorian bandstand and plenty of other visitor attractions, the beach is a mixture of pebbled beaches and low rocky cliffs, with the old harbour at the western edge of the town at the mouth of the river Yeo.

For Lionel as a young child this must have been a pleasant way to spend his spare time with friends from the school; it also had a lasting effect on his love for the seaside and what living by the coast had to offer. In later life he would retire to Dawlish a coastal town on the south coast of Devon; the sea air of Clevedon clearly left its mark with Lionel.

Clevedon in 1900; this is what the town would have looked like when Lionel attended his preparatory school

While at the school in 1879, his mother gave birth to his youngest sister in January. Tragedy was to strike the family when, on May 13, his mother died at home at Cattistock Lodge. Although her death was reported in the local newspapers it does not give the cause. I can only surmise that it was due to complications as a result from her recently giving birth. What is certain is that she left a husband and five children under the age of nine; it is hard to imagine what the effects were on the family at the time. All the local press could report was that the thoughts of the community were for the family (his mother was only 35). This was the start of a number of sad events that would affect the family over the next decade.

In 1880 the first report is given on Lionel's prowess as a cricketer, not for batting but bowling, when his under arm lobs took seven wickets in seven balls. Until his arrival at Repton there are no further references to any matches he was involved in. Then on December 23 there was a further tragedy to hit the Palairets. The following extract is taken from the *Western Gazette* of December 30, 1880:

'The family of Henry Palairet of Cattistock Lodge, have been plunged into the deepest grief, their youngest child of about two years of age, has tragically died as she was burned to death. The governess looking after the child left the room for a few minutes, on her return she found the child in flames. It appears that the child had got hold of some matches and struck one. Although the fire was put out quickly, the child was so badly burned that she died within the hour.

'That evening an inquest was held. From the evidence gathered it seems that the governess slept in the same room as the child, the child being in an adjoining cot. The nurse left the room at 8am to make breakfast for her. She had moved the matches to the opposite end of the room to the cot, thinking they were out of reach. The governess was only out of the room for five minutes, on her return she found the child on her bed covered in flames. Despite putting out the flames quickly the child died within an hour. The inquest verdict was accidental death.

Coming so soon after their mother's death this was another tragic blow to the family. The press at the time was full of sympathy towards the family; thought must also be given to the poor governess who would have had to live with this for the rest of her life, she almost certainly would have blamed herself for this terrible accident.

By 1882 Lionel's father married again, this time to Charlotte Ellen Rooke (1854-1922). The couple were married at Rampisham, Dorset. Charlotte was the second daughter of Rev FJ Rooke, Rector at Rampisham; the couple would remain together until Charlotte died 40 years later. Then in 1884 Lionel's uncle Captain Charles Palairet, now a magistrate, lost his wife in June when she was travelling by carriage (Mrs Palairet was driving) with a friend. When the horse was startled, and bolted suddenly as a result, the passenger Miss Gilbert Smith was thrown into the road and killed instantly. Mrs Palairet was also thrown into the road and was seriously injured on impact.

Captain Palairet arrived after about an hour, and his wife died almost immediately in his arms; the attending doctor was Dr Edward Grace (brother of the famous WG). The accident was at Berkeley in Gloucestershire which is near Thornbury where Dr Grace was practising. The death of Mrs Palairet resulted in her leaving a son (aged eight), and a daughter (aged two). She was also pregnant at the time of her death, and was only 28.

By 1886, Lionel had left his early education in Somerset and moved to Repton, the prestigious public school in Derbyshire. It is believed the school started in 1557 on the site of the former Repton Priory. The school has a proud history particularly in sport as well as producing many famous cricketers. It was while at Repton that Lionel developed his cricket, football and athletics, becoming a well-known personality at the school during his stay. The first known match that exists with Lionel playing is a game against Uppingham School, on June 23 and 24, 1886. Lionel batted at six for the school and made nine and 40. However the school lost a close match by nine runs; WF Whitwell took 13 wickets for Uppingham. Repton's school captain for the year was Francis Ford who played for Middlesex and five times for England. The only other innings that survives for this year is

Repton School, December 2015, looking towards the cricket field

when Lionel was run out for nought against Malvern on June 29.

Whilst researching the book I have looked on *Cricketarchive* for non-first class match scorecards Lionel played in. There are around 50 non-first class games listed; I have researched a number of other newspapers and managed to get this total up to over 150. Throughout the book I will refer to these; one thing is certain, he does not seem to have played regularly for any one club. It is clear that he enjoyed the country estate games that were played at the time. In addition there were no leagues in the south, so often he would guest for teams. As readers will soon appreciate, he played for a lot of teams until his last known game in 1926. Other sports he played when he was young, and later work and then golf, seem to have restricted his number of non-first class matches each year to generally only a handful.

By 1887 Lionel was opening the batting at Repton; against Malvern at Repton on June 7 and 8 he recorded his first known century as he made 114 and 54. The new captain of the school was Percy Farrant who like Lionel went to Oxford but would only appear in two games for the university. Sadly, he would die on board the SS Ortega off the Maldive Islands in 1921. The most attractive fixture of the year was the visit of the MCC, played at the school on June 7 and 8. The MCC's side included William Scotton (Nottinghamshire and England), Arnold Fothergill (Somerset and England), William Chatterton, (Derbyshire and England), Edmund Maynard (Derbyshire) and Henry Palairet (Lionel's father).

The school batted first made 56, with Lionel being bowled by Fothergill for 13. The MCC replied with 177 with Scotton (59) and Chatterton (64) making most of the runs. In reply Repton made 113 with Lionel being caught by his father off Scotton for 19; the school lost by an innings and eight runs.

During the summer break Lionel appeared for Lansdown (now a suburb of Bath), and Somerset Club and Ground (most of these games were played on the county ground in Taunton); he also played for the Old Reptonians, which was made up generally of former Repton pupils who toured Derbyshire for a week annually, and were led in this year by Francis Ford. Of these games his best score was 43 for Lansdown versus Knowle Park. These matches were good for Lionel's cricket development as he was playing

LCH pictured at Repton in 1888 (middle front row with bat), his brother Richard behind to the right and CB Fry back row second from left

with and against many first class cricketers. In December his uncle Lionel Oliver Bigg died, and in his will left Lionel and his siblings £2,500 each (the equivalent of £280,000 in 2016). This is a sizeable sum and clearly would set Lionel up in life.

By 1888, Lionel was made captain of the school eleven. New players to join his team were his younger brother Richard and CB Fry. Charles Fry was two years Lionel's junior, but he was already a great all-round sportsman and would go on to play 26 Tests for England. Fry was a rival at school for Lionel and he was brilliant athlete and later became a politician, writer, teacher and publisher and he also played in an FA Cup final. He would also follow Lionel to Oxford, and they played in many cricket and football teams together. A picture of the school team taken in 1888 shows the young Fry and Palairet brothers. Lionel sitting front centre gives the air of authority above his team mates.

Sadly Lionel's batting did not advance as he would have expected during the year: he made only 345 runs at 26.53, he did not top the school averages, and made only one 50; 51 against Derbyshire Friars. His lobs were useful on occasions as he took 12 wickets at 17 apiece. During the summer break he returned to the county; playing for the Old Reptonians against Buxton, he made a solid 74.

It was this year that he first played at Westbury in Wiltshire on WH Laverton's ground, and it was here that he would meet his future wife Caroline. Playing for Laverton's eleven against OG Radcliffe's eleven he was bowled by WG Grace for two but in the second innings batting at seven, he carried out his bat for a useful 29. However his team lost by eight wickets. Another important game for Lionel that year was turning out for the MCC against Lansdown in late August. Lionel opened with the great batsman William Gunn (Nottinghamshire and England), and made only 12, but he will have enjoyed playing in the same side as William Attewell (also Nottinghamshire and England) and FJ Shacklock (Nottinghamshire). While he was developing his batting his father was paying professionals such as Attewell and Fred Martin (Kent) to bowl at his sons and help develop them as cricketers.

Lionel had a much better record in 1889, his last year at Repton, as he scored 353 runs at 29.5. He also scored his second hundred, making an unbeaten 119 against Lincoln Ludlum. It was as a bowler that he made his biggest impact, as he took 56 wickets at 12.6. Despite a better batting record, Fry and his younger brother's averages were almost ten more than his. So being despite finishing on a high his batting was in the shadow of his younger brother and Fry who was two years his junior.

The school's sports day was reported in great detail in the local press. Lionel won the steeplechase and broke the school record time in winning the half mile. For the overall sports prize he lost out to Fry by ten points (410 to 400).

In June the school held its annual speech day. It filled half a page in the local *Derby Mercury* as it listed the whole day's events and prizes to individuals plus many of the notable guests. His, father, stepmother, brother and sisters were in attendance. Lionel took part in a short play called 'Les Plaideurs' taking the part of Le Souffleur; CB Fry appeared with him. As school captain he also presented some prizes and won first prize for his Greek verse. The headmaster finished with wishing the departing students well for the future. Lionel would now be looking forward to Oxford University and would have had hopes of becoming a first class cricketer.

Before starting university Lionel had time to return home to Somerset and play some more cricket. He guested for a number of sides, his best performance being 42 and 111 for WH Laverton's eleven versus Bradford Wanderers. As a result of this he was chosen to make his debut for Somerset against the MCC at Lord's on August 12, a non-first class match, scheduled over two days. He was chosen as wicketkeeper; this seems odd as he had taken so many wickets for Repton earlier in the year and of the scorecards that exist there is no evidence of him being a wicketkeeper at the school. He would though later occasionally keep for Somerset and generally seems to have been capable behind the stumps.

Batting first the MCC made only 67 with Lionel making a stumping off Ted Tyler. Somerset fared no better being skittled for 64. Lionel batting at five was bowled by Jim Phillips for two. Phillips was an Australian who came to England and played for

Middlesex, later he would become better known as an umpire determined to help rid the game of several throwers playing at the time. He called a number of bowlers for throwing, and as a result he finished several careers. Two of the cricketers he helped finish as bowlers were CB Fry and Ted Tyler. In 1900 Phillips wrote to the MCC asking for nine bowlers to be banned. He would later move to Canada and became wealthy as a mining engineer; we will hear more of Phillips later.

Getting back to the match, the MCC fared worse in their second innings making only 60 and Somerset easily knocked off the runs losing only two wickets. The match finished within a day, with Sam Woods taking 12 wickets for Somerset.

Entrance to Repton School, December 2015

Chapter three
University and plenty of sport

On conclusion of the cricket season Lionel went up to Oxford, and went to Oriel College. As he started, his family was hit by another loss. This time, it involved an uncle, the Reverend CH Palairet who was killed while crossing a road at Norton St Philip, which is halfway between Bath and Frome, where he was the vicar. Lionel often spent his holidays with him. He was struck by a horse and cart that was being driven by a young boy. In the inquest that followed, it was stated that the boy lost control of the cart and although the boy was shouting to warn passers-by, Mr Palairet still walked in front of the cart and was killed almost instantly. Accidental death was the verdict.

Although at Oxford, on the weekends Lionel travelled back to Somerset. On October 5 there is the first record of him playing football, for newly formed Bath AFC. Lionel played in their inaugural match on the North Parade Ground in Bath against Trowbridge. The side lost 9-4; the local newspaper did not record who scored the goals. Lionel played as a forward and the local press commented that he was 'a capable player noted for his swift of foot and speed of foot work'.

His prowess led in December to him being selected for a county match for Somerset versus Wiltshire at Swindon Croft. With 800 spectators in attendance Somerset won 3-2 with Lionel scoring the first for Somerset. It must be noted that football was only starting to get popular in the country. The Football League was only in its second year; professional football had only been legalised in 1885. All founder members of the league were based in the Midlands, Lancashire or Yorkshire. Some counties consisted only of a few clubs; this is well illustrated by the Wiltshire side as ten of the team played for Swindon Town. The Somerset team was made up of players from several clubs around the county.

On December 21, he played again for the county at Bristol against Gloucestershire. In front of a crowd of 2,500 (according to the *Western Daily Press*), Somerset lost a good game 6-4 with Lionel scoring twice. His brother Richard also played; he generally was a winger or midfielder and was noted for his speed and skill of passing the ball. Having looked at both careers I would say that Richard was the better player. Sadly Richard would have his knee shattered in a tackle in 1893. This injury not only finished his football career at 22, but took a year for him to recover from and as a result it restricted his movement at the crease when batting. Although Richard would probably have never emulated his brother, it seems from reports at the time, and after his retirement, that the injury hampered his career and stopped development in first class cricket. Over the next few months. Lionel continued to play for Bath at the weekends, stopping with a relative at Norton St Philip.

As the football season ended Lionel looked forward to 1890 and the prospect of making the university team and his first class debut. The local press in April looked at the prospects of the team and were not too optimistic, citing weak batting. They did however comment that Lionel should make a useful bowler with his lobs.

Lionel played a number of freshman and college games before the first fixture against the touring Australians, due early at Oxford. For Oriel he made an unbeaten 107 and 56 against Blackheath. He took eight for 37 for WN Cobbold's eleven versus Barton Brewers. Playing in the last college freshman's match he took seven wickets against the first eleven in the second innings.

It is likely that his bowling achievements resulted in his selection to play against the Australians starting on May 20 at Oxford. The university was not thought to be that strong at the time, the best player being Ernest Smith, a capable all-rounder who played for a number of teams including Yorkshire, and who would make his final first class appearance as late as 1928. Also in the side was Malcolm Jardine, a batsman, whose son Douglas would later captain England on the infamous Bodyline tour. This was co-managed by Plum Warner and Lionel's brother Richard. Like Lionel, Jardine would be famous for wearing a Harlequin cap when batting. Other key Oxford players included batsman George Wilson, an Australian by birth who would also play for Sussex. He was Lionel's best man at his wedding. The pair would lose touch as George would later return to his native country.

The game was played in poor weather throughout, windy, cold

and overcast. Winning the toss, the Australians batted first for 234 with CTB Turner top scoring with 59; for Oxford GFH Berkeley took eight for 70 and Lionel one for 48 taking the wicket of GHS Trott. By the close of play Oxford scored 63 for four. The following morning Lionel was soon in and reached six before falling lbw to Turner (known as Terror Turner). Oxford finished on 120 and followed on and could only muster 53. Lionel this time was bowled for nought by Ferris. The Australians won by an innings and 61 runs. Not a good start to his first-class career but it had to get better.

The university next entertained a Gentlemen of England side, captained by the old Middlesex cricketer AJ Webbe. Winning the toss the Gentlemen compiled a useful 261, Lionel finishing with three for 28 as he mopped up the tail. Going in early the next morning with the score on 95 for six, he added 53 with Hubert Bassett and after hitting some excellent drives he was eventually out at 193 having batted 80 minutes for his 54, hitting seven fours. In the second innings the Gentlemen ran up 321, and despite a century from WD Llewellyn the university could only muster 242, losing by 141 runs with Lionel making a solid 32. At least he had scored his maiden first-class 50 and had been a useful member of the bowling attack.

After a heavy defeat to the MCC, the university entertained a strong Lancashire team at The Parks. Thanks to 13 wickets in the match by E Smith the university won by 11 wickets (12 a side played), Lionel contributed an attractive 45 and the newspapers commented on his pleasant style, with a panache for some powerful drives and cuts. However in the return a couple of weeks later at Old Trafford the university suffered a humiliating defeat by an innings and 69 runs. Lionel had the misfortune to bag the only pair in his career. He regained some form as against Sussex at Hove, making three and 41, the university won by 86 runs. Future Hollywood actor Charles Aubrey Smith got him out in each innings; Lionel gained part revenge as he had him stumped in the first innings.

In the penultimate game before the Cambridge match, Oxford travelled to Lord's to play the MCC. Although Lionel made nought in the first innings he scored 72 in two and a quarter hours in the second, hitting seven fours and making only one faulty stroke. One newspaper described it as 'an excellent innings full of style'. Despite this Oxford were beaten by six wickets.

The final match of the season for Oxford was the annual Varsity match at Lord's. Oxford were clear underdogs. Among the Cambridge team was the captain Sam Woods, a Somerset teammate of Lionel's and at this time one of the best fast bowlers in the country. He had already played Test cricket for Australia and would later appear for England. Francis Ford, as mentioned, was a highly destructive batman and a former captain of Repton. Gregor MacGregor, Scottish born, was one of the best wicketkeepers in the country. Digby Jephson was a lob bowler but also a capable batsman who would later captain Surrey; and Stanley Jackson a fine all-rounder would later captain England.

Frederic Thesiger won the toss for Oxford and elected to bat. The side was bundled out for a paltry 42, Woods (four for 25) and Edward Streatfeild (five for 14) being almost unplayable, only Ernest Smith (22) able to cope with the bowling. Lionel was bowled for nought by Woods. To Oxford's credit they bowled well; Cambridge could make only 97. Going in a second time Oxford again struggled posting only 107, Lionel making 17, Cambridge easily reached the 54 required early on the second morning, winning by seven wickets.

This brought Lionel's first class record for the Oxford season to a close. He scored 285 runs at an average of 19, and this put him fourth in the university's batting averages; he also took 12 wickets at nearly 29. This was not the end of the season for him, as he was now free to play for Somerset. The team had already won their opening two matches of the season. His first game against Leicestershire started at Taunton on July 14 in dull weather. After electing to bat Herbert Hewett took Lionel in to open with him (for Oxford he had generally been at six to eight in the batting order). The pair opened in brilliant style adding 115 for the first wicket before Hewett was bowled. George Nichols came in at three and the pair carried on hitting the bowling to all parts; 150 was added before Lionel was bowled for 158, he was at the wicket for three and a quarter hours and hit 20 fours and ten threes. Apart from a hard chance to the keeper his innings was faultless. This innings ensured that he would now open regularly for Somerset and for a while he would have a constant opening partner in Hewett. The pair became probably the most attractive playing county cricket at that time.

Somerset went unbeaten during the season, finishing with 12 wins and a tie (against Middlesex). Lionel played in ten games scoring 408 runs at 29.14, his only other innings of note being 50 against Glamorgan at Bath, although he would often get a start. Somerset's main successes that year were the bowling of Ted Tyler and George Nichols and in latter games Sam Woods, who game after game disposed of the opposition cheaply. The main batsmen were Hewett, Nichols and Lionel. Six games were won by more than an innings.

By September, Lionel was starting his second year at Oxford. He was at weekends still travelling back to Somerset to play football. He played in the Somerset trial match, appearing for Somerset Rovers versus Central Somerset at Wells. His team lost 4-3 but the match report in the *Wells Journal* shows that Lionel scored the first and made a good impression throughout. A week later at the end of September he played for Somerset Rovers against London Casuals, losing 10-0, though the *Bath Chronicle* commented that 'he had a couple of good chances to get his team on the scoresheet'.

Lionel attended Somerset's annual general meeting in October in Taunton; his father and brother were also in attendance. The club was in high spirits as it had gone undefeated during the season. It held a celebratory dinner for all the players and officials at the club, the Mayor of Taunton also attending. Under the captaincy of Hewett and administration of HE Murray-Anderdon it was made clear that the county intended to apply to join the County Championship for 1891. County secretaries at their meeting at Lord's in December decided that Somerset would be admitted to the competition, the county having secured the minimum of 12 fixtures needed.

Back at Oxford, Lionel had now been joined by his brother Richard. Their football talents had been noticed by the Oxford authorities. Richard as well as playing in many club games in Somerset was also appearing for the top amateur club The

Corinthians. The university had a proud tradition as a football team as they had won the FA Cup in 1873-74 and had lost three other finals.

Although they were now not entering the Cup they still were a force in football, though with the development of professionalism the university was finding it harder to compete. This was evident when on November 3 they played a friendly against Football League team Aston Villa. Both Palairets were chosen, however the university was outplayed losing 7-1. The *Birmingham Daily Post* commented that 'the younger Palairet set Rhodes up for the only goal for the University with a magnificent solo run and accurate pass'.

Lionel was also playing for a team called The Crusaders, a London-based club formed in 1863 that entered the FA Cup during the 1880s and 1890s; however, they never progressed beyond the fourth round and the club is long defunct. He played a number of games for them scoring several goals. In the 1890-91 FA Cup The Crusaders lost in the first round to Birmingham St George's 2-0; it is not known if Lionel played.

Other notable games that year were against The Old Wykehamists on November 12, when the university won 5-2 with Lionel scoring the fourth; the following week the students lost 11-3 to Mr Farmer's eleven, although Lionel scored the first goal. In February he played for the university against The Crusaders; the students easily won 5-1, with Lionel scoring a goal. Later that month both Palairets played for Bath against Wells in the Somerset Challenge Cup Final; in a scrappy game Bath lost 1-0. Despite a number of games for the university and making other appearances either for Crusaders or Bath, Lionel was not chosen for the Varsity game; however Richard was. Richard was at this time a regular for The Corinthians. It has been stated that Lionel also played for The Corinthians, but the only game I have traced that he played for them was against the Barbarians in April 1892, when CB Fry and FGJ Ford were also in the team.

In addition to playing a lot of football Lionel joined the Oxford Athletic Club, and in February 1891 participated in two meetings, finishing third in the one-mile race and then winning the half mile. His athletic prowess in running resulted in his selection for the Varsity in the three-mile race. Each university had three runners. Lionel finished fourth and was caught napping on the line by AJ Fowler, an Oxford teammate; the race was won by C Elkin of Cambridge. Cambridge won six and a half to two and a half events.

With the cricket season approaching the *Belfast News* had an article about Oxford University and stated their chances of a successful season were looking rather poor. Sadly this prediction would come true as the university would not win a single first-class match.

In the warm-up games in May at Oxford, Lionel hardly scored a run; he did however take ten wickets against the Next Sixteen for the First Twelve. Later in the month he took six wickets in an innings for Oxford University against the Next Sixteen. The first match against Lancashire on May 11 was lost by an innings. The new captain was MR Jardine. The club still had Ernest Smith but the only other real new player of note was the Gloucestershire wicketkeeper WH Brain. The bowling looking particularly weak, and the game was easily lost. Another beating by the Gentlemen of England followed.

Lionel's first innings of note was 53 against H Phillipson's eleven; he also opened the bowling in each innings taking four wickets in a drawn match, after the second day was washed out. Lionel was at this time batting at number six. Heavy defeats followed against Lancashire and Sussex. Then at Lord's on June 25 Lionel made his highest score for the university, 74, giving two difficult chances at 2 and 47. Lionel made nought in the second innings and the MCC went on to win by eight wickets.

The Varsity match then followed, after one innings each Oxford trailed by 102 runs and were made to follow on. They posted 193 and left Cambridge 90 to win. However with Berkeley taking five for 20, Cambridge only just got home by two wickets. Had Cyril Foley not scored 41, Oxford may have snatched a remarkable victory. Batting at four, Lionel contributed little (two and 11). Apart from one innings Lionel had a disastrous time for the university and his bowling became less used as the season went on. Could he regain form for Somerset, who were now a first class county? With the deeds of 1890 behind them, Somerset looked forward to their first season in the Championship. The club played a number of local sides to get themselves into form before the season; many of these proved one-sided affairs, but the club hoped this would mean the players would be as prepared as they could be.

A notable player in the side was Herbert Hewett, the captain, an amateur who was a lawyer. He was a good and popular leader, though he was known for being short tempered and stubborn; this would lead to him later resigning the captaincy and quitting the club. Hewett though was a dashing and aggressive left-handed batsman, who by now was regarded as the best left-hander in the country. Sam Woods had already played a couple of times against Lionel for Cambridge. An Australian, he was sent to England by his wealthy father; although he went to Cambridge he left without a degree. He was in his prime a very fast bowler, but by 1891 was already noticeably slowing down. He would become a local character and stayed in Somerset for the rest of his life; he became an accomplished batsman in time and a long-serving, popular captain.

Another key player, Edwin (Ted) Tyler, originally from Worcestershire, was one of the few professionals at the club. He first played for the county in 1887; a slow left-arm bowler, he took 126 wickets in 1890. His wickets propelled the county to first class status; with Nichols (79 wickets) these two without doubt enabled the county to gain first-class status and should be remembered for their deeds of 1890. Other capable players included batsmen William Roe, John Challen, Vernon Hill and all-rounders Gerald Fowler and Walter Hedley, plus reliable wicketkeepers Arthur Newton and the Rev Archie Wickham. The average age of the side was only 25, so supporters of the club had reason to believe the team would perform well in the Championship and have a bright future.

Before Lionel's arrival the team had opened its season with a drawn game against Middlesex at Lord's, badly affected by the weather. Then on June 1 at the Oval, Somerset fielded all day as Surrey rattled up 449, and by the close Somerset were already struggling on 17 for two. During the night it rained heavily and the following morning on resumption the wicket was almost

SET 1892

Previous page: The team that brought Somerset to the first class ranks. Standing: HE Murray-Anderdon (honorary secretary), AE Newton, T Spencer (honorary secretary), JB Challen, WN Roe, VT Hill, T Knight (scorer). Seated: CJ Robinson, SMJ Woods, HT Hewett (captain), LCH Palairet, Tyler and Nichols. Sitting front: Capt WC Hedley and G Fowler

unplayable. Within a couple of hours Somerset had lost by an innings and 375 runs. Somerset were all out for 37 in each innings; this defeat is still the third worst in the club's history. The press were already questioning whether the West Country side was good enough, and others went further by saying it would be the team's last season in the Championship.

There was then a gap in the fixtures for over a month until, with Lionel free from his studies, he joined the team to play Lancashire at Taunton starting on July 9. Sam Woods, who had now finished at Cambridge, also joined the side, with Lionel's brother Richard, who was also making his Championship debut. Apart from one innings Lionel had hardly scored a run all season and although he made only 37 in the first innings he played well enough to suggest that he was coming into some sort of form.

Still winless the team moved to Maidstone to play Kent. Electing to bat Kent could only make 106. Lionel then played a chanceless innings of 79 to help give his side a lead of 112 which eventually led to a five wicket victory, the team's first in the Championship.

His form continued as he then hit 53, in the ten wicket victory over Gloucestershire; and in the next game making 76 in the first innings in difficult conditions, as Yorkshire thrashed Somerset by 262 runs at Taunton. The team gained revenge at Bradford winning by six wickets, Lionel making a fluent 55 in the first innings. Then on August 13, the team welcomed the county champions Surrey to Taunton for the re-match. Somerset led on first innings by 40 runs. Starting the second innings Lionel made a solid 60, which enabled his team to declare, setting Surrey 372 runs to win. Amidst great excitement Sam Woods took the last

Surrey wicket at the scheduled close of play 5.30pm, giving his team victory by 130 runs. The supporters went crazy, the scenes being recalled by many of the players years later with great affection. What it did confirm to everyone was that Somerset did belong in the Championship, with Lionel also playing his part.

In the next game Lionel scored exactly 100 against Gloucestershire at Cheltenham, in three and a half hours; the press described it as 'a fine innings with patience and strong defence'. One of his hits was into the pavilion crowd off Dr WG Grace. Lionel added 138 for the second wicket with JB Challen (79). Lionel's faultless maiden first-class century included six fours and six threes, ending the ball after when he was caught at point. Somerset bowled Gloucestershire for 25 in their first innings with Woods and Tyler sharing the wickets, and won easily by an innings and 130.

The season concluded with Somerset winning five and losing six of their Championship games, putting them sixth with a minus one record; this form of deciding the Championship remained in place throughout his Somerset career. Surrey were champions for the second successive year. Lionel finished the season with 821 runs at 24.14, including a century and seven fifties; this marked a great advancement in his reputation as an opening batsman. For Somerset he topped the averages scoring 560 at 31.1.

As the season closed Lionel was named among a team raised by Lord Hawke to tour the United States and Canada to play eight matches. The first two would be regarded as first-class. The tour would mean he would miss two months of his studies. The university authorities did not take too well to this, and within a week of the team being announced, Lionel had to withdraw as Oxford refused him a sabbatical. In the event Sam Woods took his place and the tour ended with Hawke's side being unbeaten and winning seven games; Somerset's captain Herbert Hewett also went. This would be the nearest Lionel would ever get to touring abroad; he did turn down two offers to tour Australia in 1894-95 and 1903-04, but could not go due to work and family commitments.

There was happier news, as later in September he was appointed captain of the cricket team for 1892 at Oxford. So it was back to his studies but also to play some football. Oxford went to Trent Bridge to play a strong Notts County team that had finished third in the Football League; the undergraduates were heavily beaten 8-0. Oxford's team included CB Fry who had now arrived from Repton; he was to strengthen the cricket team. Both Palairets were singled out for their play by local reporters with favourable comments.

In late November Oxford had a friendly with Wolverhampton Wanderers at Molineux. Wolves had just finished fourth in the Football League; according to the Birmingham Post, Wolverhampton put out a fairly weak team to play the undergraduates. Oxford were still thrashed 6-1; however the *Birmingham Daily Post* for December 1 did state that both Palairet brothers made some good runs together. The matches with Wolves and Notts County were showing a growing gap between amateur sides and the professionals. Lionel was again overlooked for the Varsity football match with Cambridge; Richard did play and scored a goal as Oxford won 5-2. Richard was clearly the better footballer and during the season 1892-93 was also still a regular for The Corinthians.

Lionel also competed for Oxford in a number of athletic events in March and April, and was in the trial for the university selection against Cambridge. However in the one mile he finished sixth, and in the three mile he was seventh out of nine. As a result he was not selected. These performances seem to have ended his athletics career, as there are no more known records of him participating in any athletic meetings.

Lionel did have the cricket season to look forward to and his new role as captain. Although the bowling was still fairly weak, the batting was bolstered by some new promising players most notably CB Fry, Frank Phillips (who would later play for Somerset) and Somerset teammate Vernon Hill. Lionel started well in the warm-up games hitting two centuries for his college in the same week; however in the university trial games he yet again struggled for runs, though he did take a number of wickets. Oxford opened their first-class season with a home game against a Gentlemen of England side; the university was well beaten by ten wickets. However Lionel took five for 98 with his lobs and in the first innings he top scored with 49 batting at four.

Lancashire were next to visit The Parks. Oxford gained a brilliant victory by seven runs. Winning the toss Oxford batted first, and Lionel opening was bowled by Arthur Mold for nought. The undergraduates could only make 132. Lionel then opened the bowling with Berkeley and took four for 27 to help dismiss Lancashire for 88, gaining a valuable lead of 44 runs. In the second innings batting at four, Lionel made a brilliant 57, an innings ended by a brilliant catch by Frank Sugg in the long field. Despite this Oxford could only make 105. Again Lionel opened the bowling and capped a brilliant match by taking four for 52 as Oxford just scraped home amidst scenes of great excitement.

Although Oxford were beaten by Surrey by an innings in the next match, in the second innings Lionel and Jones added 83 in 50 minutes, as both of them went for the bowling; however once the partnership was broken the side were skittled for 128. Early in June Somerset visited Oxford. Lionel would have been pleased as the university easily won by seven wickets; his unbeaten 43 in the second innings included hitting Nichols for four successive boundaries in one over. He finished the match with a drive out of the ground for six.

In the return game with Lancashire at Manchester, the northern county gained revenge, winning by an innings. Lionel took six for 84 which was to be his best career bowling; he claimed some useful scalps such as Johnny Briggs. He also shared the wicket-keeping duties with Jardine; so he had a busy match.

In the next game at Hove against Sussex, the undergraduates again won a close game, this time by ten runs. Lionel in the first innings scored 51 which was described by the press as 'brilliant' and in the second innings made a two and a half hour, unbeaten 75. He also then took three for 51 including the key wickets of Marlow and Wilson.

Oxford went into the Varsity game on a good run, and although still underdogs knew they were capable of beating Cambridge. As for Lionel, he had already been on the losing side in the previous two years. Winning the toss Oxford posted a good score of 365 thanks to centuries from Jardine and Hill. Cambridge were then made to follow on as they were all out for 160. By the close of the second day they had reached 314 for five, and the following morning the innings closed for 388, leaving Oxford 184 to win. With the score at 98 for four Cambridge had an outside chance of winning; at this point Lionel and Fry added 71 in 50 minutes. Fittingly Lionel made the winning hit as he finished on 71 which included 11 fours; Oxford had won by five wickets. The match was watched by more than 40,000 spectators over the three days. This capped a good season for Oxford as they beat three first-class counties and won the Varsity match for the first time since 1887.

Lionel's performances for the university resulted in him being selected for the Gentlemen versus Players match at Lord's starting on July 4. This honour shows the growing reputation he had as a player. Sadly the Gentlemen were well beaten by an innings. Lionel batting at five could only make 10 and 13. He was retained in the team for the second of these games, at The Oval starting on July 11. This time he opened in both innings, faring better making 30 and 22 but again his team were well beaten by ten wickets.

As with the previous two years, the end of the academic year meant he could join Somerset for the rest of the season. In a major change in the Championship, all counties played each other home and away so everyone played 16 games. At this point in the season Somerset had played four matches, with one win and three defeats.

Lionel had played earlier against Middlesex without success, but he joined the team at Bristol for the match against Gloucestershire starting on July 14. Winning the toss Gloucestershire (who were without WG Grace who had a bad knee) scored 202. By the close Somerset had progressed to 125 for four, with Lionel unbeaten on 75. The *Western Daily Press* described his innings as, 'hard hitting, clean and well timed and his batting was applauded each time by the home crowd'. The following morning, he completed his century, and fell shortly afterwards for 104 without giving a chance. This helped Somerset to 313; Somerset went on to win easily by seven wickets. The team's form continued as Lancashire were then beaten by four wickets at Taunton, Lionel and Hewett making fifties in the second innings. Somerset were to make it three wins in a row when Sussex arrived at Taunton, on July 21. After an even first innings, Somerset were set 232 to win. With Hewett accompanying Lionel to the wicket the pair rattled up 125 for the first wicket in only 66 minutes, Hewett making 84. Lionel continued and was third out at 185 having made 70, scoring ten fours and making no mistake. Somerset's victory soon followed as they would only lose a further wicket. There was a large crowd at Taunton at the finish and the team won amidst great excitement.

Somerset made it four in a row as they beat Kent at Taunton; Lionel had a poor game scoring one and none. The run was broken by Lancashire at Manchester, in a sensational match completed in one day. Having lost the first day due to rain, the game started at 11.15am on the second morning and would be all over by 6.15pm. Somerset elected to bat and were dismissed for 88, having been at one point 60 for one; the drying wicket became increasingly difficult to score runs on. Lancashire replied with 116, so Somerset entered the second innings with a deficit of 28. Lionel could only watch as Briggs and Mold ran through the side, as he carried out his bat for 22 out of 58. Lancashire easily knocked off the 31 to win.

A return to form meant an easy win at Sheffield against Yorkshire. But then coming back to Taunton the team were well beaten by the eventual champions Surrey. In the first innings Lionel scored a chanceless 79, just helping to avoid the follow-on. The *Morning Post* reported: 'It would be almost impossible to overpraise the nerve, and skill of his innings for in the whole duration of his innings of two and three quarter hours, in difficult batting conditions he did not give a chance.' His innings of a six and ten fours ended with a fine catch in the deep. During the match he completed 1,000 first class runs for the season, following Arthur Shrewsbury and Andrew Stoddart, the first time he had completed this feat.

After an innings victory over Nottinghamshire, in which Ted Tyler had match figures of 15 for 96, Somerset then beat Middlesex by 70 runs at Taunton. At this point in the season Somerset were placed third, having won eight matches and losing five thus having a plus three points total, well behind Surrey

LCH and Herbie Hewett (right) showing their club record stand of 346, against Yorkshire at Taunton in 1892. The photo was taken well after the match, so postcards of the achievement could be sold

and Nottinghamshire. Somerset's return game with Yorkshire at Taunton started on August 25. Electing to bat and starting their innings in good weather, Yorkshire batted most of the day compiling a good score of 299. With less than 40 minutes to the close Hewett and Lionel opened and immediately went after the bowling; by the close they had 78 on the board. Lionel had been missed at the wicket when 28 and this drop would be severely punished.

The second day witnessed some incredible batting. The pair put up the century stand in 65 minutes; Hewett reached his century in two hours; and shortly afterwards 200 went up and Lionel's hundred was attained 20 minutes later. The scoring rate actually increased as the third century took only an hour. Eventually at 3pm, Hewett was bowled by Peel for 201. The pair had added 346 runs scoring at 100 runs per hour. The partnership broke the world record for any wicket at the time, beating Dr WG Grace and BB Cooper's stand of 283 set in 1868. This partnership is still the Somerset record for the first wicket. Lionel was eventually out at 372, having batted three hours and 35 minutes and hitting one six and 19 fours. Somerset continued to pile up runs, Walter Hedley made 102 as the side was all out for 592 just before the close. Sadly, the last day was washed out robbing the county of probable victory, but the partnership was the talking point for the press for months to come.

The bad weather continued as Somerset's last two games were virtually washed out. This concluded the season for Somerset, who finished third in the Championship. They would not equal this position again until 1958, and would not beat this until 2001 when they finished second. Somerset to 2015 have not won the Championship though they have been runners-up three times.

The cricket season was not quite finished for Lionel; he was selected in a scratch match for West of England versus East of England at Portsmouth. This time he was on the winning side, making useful scores of 33 and 25 and his team won by 48 runs. Sam Woods took 13 for 109. Lionel's final game of the season was his third appearance for the Gentlemen against the Players, at Hastings. Starting on September 12 the match was drawn; having made the Players follow on the Gentlemen were glad to come away with a draw. Lionel made a useful 38 in the second innings.

In a review of the season Lionel had made 1,343 runs at 31.97 and taken 30 wickets at 24.13. It was surprising that after his successes for the university, that Hewett hardly used his lobs for Somerset. In November he was again re-elected as captain of Oxford for 1893. The following month Somerset held the annual meeting at the London Hotel in Taunton. Despite a successful season on the field the club made a loss of £98 (£11,000 in 2016 money); reports of losses would become common leading up to 1914. At the meeting both he and Hewett were presented with miniature silver bats in recognition of their 346 partnership against Yorkshire.

In addition the public could buy a postcard of the pair of them in front of the scoreboard which showed the opening stand. This photograph was taken well after the game and was purely for public sales. During the meeting Lionel was elected to the Somerset committee; his uncle Major Palairet was also on the committee.

Although going back to his studies for his final year, Lionel was still playing football at the weekends, for Dorchester Town. The club was formed in 1880 and were to join the Dorset League in 1896.

In March 1893 the press stated that William Attewell (of Nottinghamshire and England) was being employed solely by the Palairets to improve their batting. On April 8, Lionel as a footballer turned out for Dorset against Somerset, the match ended a draw, 0-0; Lionel's brother was the referee. Before the university season, there were the usual freshman matches against the university eleven; these games were used not only as practice but to see what new talent was available. Lionel batted steadily in these games making two fifties and also taking wickets steadily.

One game in particular, First Eleven versus Next Sixteen played on May 11 and 12 was worthy of mention. The First Eleven scored 533 and the Next Sixteen replied with 427. WH Brain who went in last for the First Eleven made 92. New players who were expected to do well included GJ Mordaunt, HDG Leveson-Gower, LCV Bathurst, GB Raikes and WH Brain; the batting looked stronger than the previous year.

The first game followed shortly afterwards at Oxford, against Lancashire; the game ended in a draw as most of the final day was washed out. Lancashire were in a good position and probably would have won. Lionel made a useful 35 in the second innings. The following day the university entertained the Gentlemen of England captained by AJ Webbe. Again the weather washed out most of the final day. The university had the better of the game scoring 321 with Lionel making a fluent 74 on a difficult pitch, making the visitors follow on, although in their second innings the Gentlemen made 318 for seven when play ended.

Lionel missed the next game with Somerset due to a cold. Somerset gained revenge for the previous year by winning easily by nine wickets. Hewett's 94 and Tyler's 11 wickets did most of the work for the visitors. Lionel was fit for the visit of the Australians; in a close game Australia won by 19 runs. Oxford's last two wickets put on 58 and nearly caused a surprise victory. Lionel with three and 27 had a quiet match. Oxford's poor start to the season continued as they were well beaten by the MCC and Lancashire, each by an innings.

Lionel on June 26 played for Arthur Shrewsbury's eleven against the Australians at Nottingham, a benefit match for Shrewsbury. The strong team included Dr WG Grace, AE Stoddart, William Gunn, Shrewsbury and WW Read among the first six in batting. Lionel went in at four. Going in with the score at 170 for two he batted 90 minutes for his 71; he added 109 for the third wicket with William Gunn. His team posted 416 and the Australians replied feebly with 120 and 143 to lose by an innings and 153. Yorkshire's Bobby Peel took match figures of 11 for 110. As a result of this game Lionel missed the university's match against Sussex; the students were well beaten again by ten wickets.

In the final game before the Varsity clash, Lionel played as wicket-keeper in the return game with the MCC at Lord's. Again Oxford were easily beaten by eight wickets; as in 1891 the university had not won a game on the eve of its most important fixture with Cambridge. Unlike Oxford, Cambridge had won their first four games; though they had faltered a little, they had just thumped the MCC. The team included some good new players who were to make their mark on the first-class game including

KS Ranjitsinjhi, CM Wells, AJL Hill and AO Jones.

Oxford based on form and, it seemed, on ability were not given much chance. The game started on July 3 in front of an estimated 20,000. By the end of the first day each side had completed an innings, with Cambridge leading by 76; Lionel's 32 was his team's top score. The second day too was played in front of 20,000 with Cambridge making 254, setting Oxford 319 to win. Oxford needed to bat well to have any chance. Sadly Lionel fell for two and this started a procession as Oxford were routed for 64, so losing the game by the huge margin of 266.

This was a disappointing end for Lionel and Oxford; for the second time in three years the team had failed to win a first-class match. This was not quite the end for Lionel at Oxford, as the following week they played a non-first class match against Dublin University; sadly they even lost this match by eight wickets, with Lionel signing off his Oxford career with scores of six and four.

As his university time was coming to an end, The *Taunton Courier* announced in June that on completion of his studies, Lionel was to study electrical engineering in Taunton. It was of local opinion that he was expected to settle in the area as a result. Within a few days it was also announced in The Bristol Mercury that he was to marry the second daughter of WH Laverton: Caroline Mabel, born in 1871 and from Westbury. Lionel had met her through playing on her father's specially built cricket ground. Mabel was from a large family - six of her brothers were cricketers - and her family were well known mill owners in the Westbury area.

Her father William Henry Laverton (1845-1935) had in his time been a Conservative parliamentary candidate, a magistrate, High Sheriff and chairman of magistrates for Wiltshire. A close friend of WG Grace, he helped cricket in the county of Wiltshire immensely and a number of his sons turned out for them.

After setting his personal life and professional career in motion, Lionel then joined the Somerset team for the rest of the season. Somerset had lost all six of its Championship games heavily. The county badly needed the Palairets and Vernon Hill back to change the team's fortunes. His first game was against Kent at Taunton, starting July 10. Although the game ended in a draw due to the weather, Lionel carried his bat on a difficult wicket making 51 out of 122; he batted 195 minutes without giving a chance.

The team then moved to the Oval and beat Surrey by 39 runs; a surprise first win as Surrey were the current champions, however the side was ageing and would slip to fifth place. The title would be won by Yorkshire by a clear five points, the start of a long successful period for Yorkshire. In the match Lionel failed in both innings. A draw followed against Lancashire; however, had the game been completed, Somerset would have probably won.

On July 20, the Australians started their tour game at Taunton. On the first morning following overnight heavy rain, the umpires decided that due to the wet pitch it was unlikely play could start until late afternoon. However Hewett and Blackham, the Australian captain, agreed to abandon play for the day. The visiting team he left the ground for a picnic in the Quantock Hills. However, several thousand spectators stayed and voiced their frustration; some had travelled over 100 miles to see the day's play; many thought play could have commenced and it now had turned bright and sunny.

As a result of this pressure from spectators and the Somerset committee, the umpires declared that play could start at 2pm. The problem was the Australians had left for the hills. A man on horseback was sent to look for them, found them, and the team arrived back at 4pm. At 4.20pm the game started. By the close Somerset were all out for 119, with Lionel top scorer with 30. It was not known at the time but this incident would cause the loss of Herbert Hewett as a player to Somerset. On the second day after bowling the Australians for 107, Somerset broke down badly in the second innings being dismissed for 64, and lost easily by six wickets.

With the events at Taunton being temporarily forgotten, Somerset travelled to Liverpool for the game against Lancashire and again suffered a thrashing, this time by 230 runs. Coming back to Taunton to play Middlesex starting on August 7, Lionel was demoted to number seven as he was hardly scoring a run. This demotion worked; the team ran up 380 with Lionel making 91, although dropped twice (on 19 and 40). He made two drives out of the ground during his innings. Although they made Middlesex

Herbie Hewett, Lionel's first captain and one of the best left-handers in the country. Sadly a disagreement with the Somerset committee resulted him in leaving the club at the end of 1893

follow on, Somerset in the end only just held on to a draw thanks to an undefeated half century by WC Hedley.

Restored back to opening the innings for the next game, opening with Hedley (Hewett had demoted himself to four), in an hour and 35 minutes Lionel scored 73. His innings was again marred by two chances, the first before he had scored, being dropped in the slips. John Challen made 108 in the second innings but Sussex's last pair hung on for a draw.

In the return with Gloucestershire at Cheltenham, Somerset recorded their second victory of the season by defeating their neighbours by 127 runs. In the second innings Lionel made 72 in two hours and ten minutes, but gave three chances, the first on two being an easy one. So although he was contributing some useful scores, he was regularly giving chances each innings.

Somerset finished the season with innings wins over Nottinghamshire at Taunton, with Hewett making 120, and in the final game, the return with Gloucestershire. Hewett this time made 112, sharing an opening stand of 163 with Lionel who made 53. Hewett actually scored 107 before lunch. This final victory was the county's fourth of the season but it only meant them finishing above Gloucestershire in the final Championship table.

Hewett had played his last game for the county; he is the only player to have hit hundreds in his last two Championship innings. At the end of the season he resigned the captaincy and announced he would not continue to play for the county. The club tried to keep him, and offered a testimonial for 1894, however in vain. Hewett was a stubborn man but it's sad that at 29 his career was virtually at an end. In 1892 he was the only left-handed batsman to score 1,000 runs in the County Championship; he was certainly one of the most entertaining batsmen to watch, and deprived himself as well as Somerset of many more innings.

He did turn out occasionally for other teams, including on a tour to South Africa, but by 1896 he left the first-class game for good. He was a barrister by profession, so he carried on his work and he died in 1921 at 56. He played fifty matches for Somerset scoring 2,592 runs at 30.85. Although Lionel did not attend the funeral, the Palairet family sent a wreath.

The season for Lionel was rather disappointing; in his final year at Oxford his side failed to win a game and with the bat he never showed any consistency; he scored 871 runs at 26.39 without a century. He rarely was called upon to bowl. Despite this he was chosen by *Wisden* as one of the five cricketers of the year, the others being Hewett, AE Stoddart and SW Scott (Middlesex) and WW Read (Surrey). All the players chosen were batsman. Going on statistics Lionel certainly did not deserve it for his efforts on the field during the season. However the faith placed in his abilities were not misplaced; he would show to in time to be at the front rank of amateur batsmen in the country for a number of years.

With the season over Lionel continued to play football; he played for Oxford Cygnets. This move caused the press to comment on him moving from the Dorchester club, however by Christmas Lionel had moved back to play for Bath. In November he attended a meeting at Taunton. The Somerset cricket club committee agreed that Sam Woods would be the new captain for 1894. He would stay as captain until 1906, a true character, who initially was a fine fast bowler but as his powers diminished he became a capable hard-hitting batsman, very popular with the public and his team.

In December, Lionel returned to Oxford to receive his BA honours in Arts, then on Christmas Day he turned out to play county football for Somerset versus Gloucestershire at Midsomer Norton. With nearly 2,000 in attendance the result was a 2-2 draw with Lionel scoring the first goal. As 1894 started Lionel was elected onto the Taunton Cricket Club committee (Taunton Cricket Club shared the ground with the county team) and he also announced that he was to marry on July 5. With his life rapidly changing this would be the last season he would play regular football.

Chapter four
Marriage, family, work and Somerset

Lionel started the 1894 season with a few minor games, his best being 72 playing for Sam Woods's Bridgwater against Glastonbury. The county started the season with a heavy loss to Middlesex at Lord's but then won a thrilling game at Hove by one wicket, Lionel not contributing much in either game.

Somerset then travelled to Oxford to play the university. His brother and CB Fry were in the undergraduates' side. After an innings apiece Somerset trailed by 131 runs, Lionel though had taken four for 49 and among his wickets was Fry. Batting a second time Lionel showed fine form, however early on the third day the side had slipped to 203 for seven, when JA Gibbs (75) helped Lionel add 129. Lionel was then dismissed for an excellent 181 in three hours 45 minutes, which included 24 fours. He and Gibbs saved the game.

He took this form into the next county game at Canterbury against Kent; he made solid contributions of 60 and 61 as Somerset won a hard-fought game by three wickets. Sam Woods' match figures of 12 for 172 were the most significant performance. Somerset then recorded an easy win over Gloucestershire. Lionel then played against the South Africans in a non-first class game and produced two fine innings 69 and 82, as Somerset easily beat the visitors by nine wickets.

Lionel married Caroline Mabel Laverton at the parish church in Westbury. A number of newspapers gave a detailed account of the wedding, listed all the gifts and all who attended. There were several hundred guests, with many sirs and ladies named. After the wedding the couple caught a train from Westbury to Dunster in Somerset, for their honeymoon, a driving tour in Devon.

After his honeymoon, Lionel returned to county cricket, for Somerset against Nottinghamshire at Trent Bridge. Although the team lost a closely fought game by 21 runs, the match would be remembered for two innings: a brilliant unbeaten century by William Gunn but also Lionel's 119. Set 224 to win, Lionel entered the chase at nine for two. He immediately went after the bowling; wickets though kept tumbling at the other end and the side was reduced to 99 for seven. He then found useful partners in Hill and Evans and the score reached 152 for nine, when last man Wickham joined him. Wickham was not known as a batsman, being known by his colleagues as 'Snickham'. However he stayed whilst Lionel upped the tempo. The pair added 50 (Wickham made four), when it seemed possible that Somerset might win. However Lionel was given out lbw as he tried to turn a ball to leg. His faultless innings of three hours ten minutes included 12 fours.

The next game against Lancashire was finished in a single day. Electing to bat on a damp wicket Somerset were bundled out for 31 in 50 minutes. Lancashire replied with 231 with Frank Sugg scoring 105 in 80 minutes. Somerset in reply made 132 largely due to Lionel's 69 in 80 minutes. Mold though had the last say as he finished with match figures of 13 for 60.

Moving from Manchester to Huddersfield for the fixture against Yorkshire, Somerset had the indignity of suffering another defeat within a day. Somerset's combined two innings lasted less than three hours and Yorkshire's 173 was enough for an innings victory. No other side has ever lost back to back county games in a day.

The team's fortunes did not improve until the visit of Kent at Taunton, on July 30. After Kent made Somerset follow on, Lionel top scored with 51 as Somerset made 230, setting the visitors 121 to win. Somerset skittled them for 83. This improved form continued as Sussex were well beaten by 110 runs, Lionel contributing a useful 58. The next four games produced two draws and two defeats with a runs of low scores by Lionel. The last county match produced another victory over Gloucestershire, by five wickets; Lionel again contributed little with the bat. Somerset won six and lost seven of their 16 games. This meant an improvement to sixth in the Championship. Lionel then played in a few minor matches, scoring 103 for Taunton against George Nichol's Moonlight team at Taunton on September 6.

Lionel had one more first-class match before the season was finished, as he was selected to represent the Gentlemen of the South against Players of the North at Lord's from September 17. The game ended in a draw with Lionel being dismissed in each innings by Essex's Walter Mead for three and 36. Lionel finished 14th in the national averages having scored 969 runs at 29.36.

At the end of the month he was elected as a vice-president of Taunton Cricket Club; also that month it was noted in the press that he enjoyed staghound meetings. In an interview in 1901 he was asked what his favourite sport was. Surprisingly he said foxhunting; however within a few years, golf took over his spare time and definitely became his main passion. It seems Lionel concentrated on his professional career, building a life for himself and his wife. By Christmas she was expecting their first child.

A few changes during the winter affected the Championship. The method of deciding the Championship from 1895 to 1909, was changed on the basis of one point for each victory, one point deducted for each defeat, the final order being decided by the greatest proportion of points gained to games completed. Surrey were eventual champions winning 17 games and losing four, this gave them a net of 13 points or 61.9 per cent (13/21) of points obtained for completed matches; drawn games were ignored.

Secondly having agreed in 1894 the Championship would be expanded to fourteen teams from 1895 Derbyshire, Hampshire, Essex, Leicestershire and Warwickshire were now admitted. For Somerset this meant an increase of two games to 18; it meant they would only play against Essex and Hampshire of the newcomers and they dropped the fixture with Nottinghamshire; the side would also play Oxford and Cambridge universities.

Lionel started the 1895 season playing for the county against the Colts. He made a useful 36 and took five for 43 with his lobs. The first-class season started with a visit to Cambridge to play the undergraduates. Somerset were well beaten by seven wickets. During the first innings Lionel made 98, but it was Frank Mitchell's 191 that stole the show along with Sam Woods hitting a brilliant 180 in the second innings in a losing cause.

The first Championship match was to become part of history, as the team travelled to Bristol to play Gloucestershire, starting on May 16. Captain of Gloucestershire was the greatest all-rounder of his time WG Grace. Aged 46, his recent form over the past few years suggested that his best days were over. However he had started the season in fine form and he arrived at the match with 99 first-class hundreds. The match started well for Somerset. Lionel with Gerald Fowler put on 205 for the first wicket; Lionel made a solid 80 while Fowler made 118 (his only first-class hundred). The batting broke down badly and the side collapsed to 303 all out; Grace bowled 45 overs taking five for 87. By the close of play Gloucestershire had reached 58 for two with WG on 32.

The second day the Doctor went on to 288 without giving a chance, hitting 38 fours. Somerset went on to lose the match by nine wickets. Grace went onto score 1,000 runs in May, finishing the season with 2,346 runs at 51 with nine centuries. His performances were followed with great interest throughout the season.

Before the next county game Somerset travelled to Oxford and the undergraduates enjoyed a close win in an exciting game by one wicket. However it was the start of Somerset's second innings which caused a lot of comment in the press. With Somerset trailing by 85 runs after first innings, Sam Woods and Lionel opened the innings. They both batted like the game was a modern T20 match. The pair added 50 in only 14 minutes, eventually adding 73 in only 25 minutes; the hundred went up after 50 minutes. Lionel's share of the stand was 28 whilst Woods (first out) made 48.

The county's first victory of the summer should have been against Hampshire, however after making Hampshire follow on they went on to lose by a narrow margin of 11 runs. Somerset's first innings of 221 relied heavily on Lionel's 96, made at almost a run a minute. Hampshire were then skittled by Tyler and Woods and followed on. Some solid Hampshire batting meant Somerset needed 188 runs and after reaching 166 for five victory seemed assured; however the last five wickets fell for only ten runs.

The next game against Middlesex at Lord's proved to be a personal triumph for the Palairet brothers, a match played for the benefit of Thomas Mycroft, a much esteemed member of the ground staff. Starting on June 3, with Somerset electing to bat, the innings opened with Lionel and Gerald Fowler; the pair put on 49 in half an hour before Fowler was bowled. The Palairet brothers then came together and soon showed complete mastery over the bowling. Lionel made many hits by clean driving along the ground (the press noted this was unusual for him). At lunch the score had already reached 176 for one, with Lionel reaching 74 and Richard on 41.

After lunch the partnership continued until the score reached 226, with Lionel being caught at the wicket for 109 off one of Evan Nepean's slows. He was at the wicket almost three hours; the press called his innings as 'almost faultless'. His younger brother went on to his maiden first-class hundred before falling for 106. Middlesex drew with only two wickets left and in a hopeless position. On the first day when the Palairets batted, almost 18,000 spectators watched, which was stated to be a record for Lord's at that time.

However, defeats then followed against Sussex, Surrey and Essex before the rot was stopped in the return game with Hampshire at Southampton. Somerset at this point were bottom of the Championship having lost five games (including the Varsity games, seven). Due to work commitments Lionel had been missing since the Sussex game. He would return to the side and be part of one of the county's worst ever weeks.

The first of these games was at Taunton against Essex starting on July 11. Having made 246, Essex then ran up 692 with three players scoring a century and a fourth making 99. The game was lost by an innings and 317 runs early on the third day; this remains the club's fifth ever heaviest defeat. On the third day Lionel's wife Caroline gave birth to a baby girl, the couple named her Evelyn Mabel though she would always be known as 'Molly'. The following year the couple would have a son Henry Edward; this would complete the Palairet family.

Two days later Lancashire visited Taunton. Electing to bat, Archie MacLaren opened with Albert Ward. MacLaren was nearly bowled in the first over by Tyler but after this, it was to be all Lancashire. The opening pair put on 141 until Ward was caught for 64. Arthur Paul then joined his captain and the pair would add 363 before Lionel had Paul caught in the outfield for 177. At the close of play MacLaren had reached 289 and Lancashire 555 for three; Lancashire had even sent in a nightwatchman.

The following day MacLaren passed the previous world record score of WG Grace's 344 made in 1876. He eventually fell for

424 (with a six and 62 fours), and the side was eventually all out for 801. Lionel had the best figures of four for 133; poor Ted Tyler's combined analysis for these two games was six for 427 off 119.3 overs. Not surprisingly Somerset made little fight of the game, losing by an innings and 452; this remains the club's heaviest defeat. MacLaren's record score in England was not beaten until Brian Lara's undefeated 501 for Warwickshire against Durham in 1994.

These defeats kept the club firmly at the bottom of the Championship. This run continued with defeats to Yorkshire and Kent; Lionel was missing for both. However the month of August would see the club fortune's change dramatically.

The run started with the arrival of Middlesex to the county ground on August 5. Back in the team Lionel played a remarkable innings. He reached his fifty out of 65 minutes and his century out of 155 in 115 minutes. He batted altogether for 140 minutes and carried his bat through the innings for 113 out of 172. He scored 17 fours and batted in almost faultless style, his only chance being just before the innings was closed. Due to the weather the game was unfinished but at least the run of defeats was halted.

In the next game against Sussex, again at Taunton, Lionel produced another fine display hitting up 91 out of a total of 220 as the county romped home by ten wickets. It was also a personal triumph for Tyler who had match figures of 15 for 95. Somerset then beat Kent by seven wickets with useful knocks of 44 and 59 from Lionel.

The county then entertained Surrey, the eventual champions for the fifth time in six years. Lionel top scored in the first innings making 64 as the county struggled to 168. Tyler then took all ten Surrey wickets for 49, as Somerset gained a first innings lead of 29. In the second innings Lionel (26) and Fowler put on 66 for the first wicket; however, after they were separated Tom Richardson took seven for 67 as the county slumped to 141 all out. Surrey only required 171 to win, but fine bowling and poor running (there were three run outs) saw them fall short by 53 runs.

Yorkshire then visited Taunton and in a close contest the southern county triumphed again. Facing a first innings deficit of 61, Lionel then played one of his best ever innings for the county as he held the side together with a brilliant 165 in four hours, with 24 boundaries; he gave only one difficult chance when 56. Set 295 to win, Yorkshire were going well reaching 173 for two when Tyler then performed the hat-trick; this changed the match and Somerset won by 29 runs, Tyler finishing with match figures of 14 for 247.

Somerset continued with a 57-run win over Gloucestershire, Lionel making 68 in the second innings; this meant the county had won its last five matches. This run lifted the team to a respectable equal eighth in the table, the main two contributors being Lionel and Ted Tyler. Although Lionel scored 1,313 runs at 46.89 which put him fifth in the national averages, he started to miss matches due to work commitments; this trend would continue and work would increasingly start to gain the upper hand over time.

In reviewing the season in *Wisden* the editor had this to say about Lionel's batting:

'Most of Mr Palairet's triumphs were gained at Taunton, but though the ground is unquestionably one of the easiest in the country, the Old Oxonian on more than one occasion playing with conspicuous skill and success under disadvantageous conditions when the wicket had been badly affected by rain.'

In August he actually scored 648 runs, and as can be seen was not just a good player on good tracks; over the years in many instances he played on difficult surfaces with great care and skill, still with the ability to score runs at a healthy rate. It was really 1895 that he came to the front as one of the country's leading batsman.

In November Lionel attended the annual Somerset meeting and was elected to the Somerset committee; the purchase of the ground was also confirmed. His father as ever was also present.

Lionel started the 1896 season playing for Taunton; on May 2 he made 13 against Bridgwater, dismissed by a young fast bowler called George Gill, who would make his Somerset debut the following year but at the end of 1902 suddenly left to play for his county of birth Leicestershire. With Woods and Nichols less effective as bowlers, the county had bolstered the bowling by engaging Ernest Robson as one of the few county professionals that they could afford. He was now eligible to play for the county. Robson was a Yorkshireman who had played for Cheshire until 1894. He would stay with the county until 1923 playing in 424 matches. He would score over 10,000 runs and take over 1,000 wickets, as a most reliable member of the team.

On May 4, the county started its annual pre-season match to find new players within the county; so L Palairet's eleven played SMJ Woods' eleven. Lionel was dismissed in each innings again by Gill. However during the second innings Lionel made 51 and added 135 in 55 minutes with Robson. By making 102 Robson had followed up a hundred he had made earlier playing in the match with Lionel against Bridgwater. Committee members must have been pleased with Robson's early form.

Somerset began the season with an easy win at Bristol over Gloucestershire, Tyler with match figures of 14 for 122 and Woods making a century being the chief contributors. It was then back to Taunton to entertain Yorkshire. Electing to bat Somerset ran up 323 with Lionel making 113. However Yorkshire led by 77 on the first innings and were to complete a five wicket victory late on the third day.

The next match against Middlesex at Lord's was not for 12 days and on the morning of the second day, he received a telegram to return home due an incident in the family. I have been unable to ascertain what this was; in his absence the Somerset team easily lost by an innings. He returned for the next game at Brighton against Sussex. In a high-scoring game Somerset made Sussex follow on; however Sussex then made 525 for four, with a double hundred from Billy Newham and centuries from old Billy Murdoch and Ranjitsinjhi. Playing for a draw Somerset slumped to 21 for six within 45 minutes; a defeat now looked likely as two hours still remained. Lionel though found useful partners in Hedley and Robinson as Somerset closed on 122 for seven, Lionel making an unbeaten 83.

After missing the next couple of weeks he returned to the team to play Hampshire, starting on June 15. The weather badly affected the game and Somerset's 337 for nine was as far as the game reached. Spread over two days Lionel batted four hours and 25 minutes making an unbeaten 147.

After two more heavy defeats, he was chosen to represent the Gentlemen versus Players at the Oval starting on July 6. In an exciting game the Gentlemen won by one wicket, however Lionel could only muster one and eight. On conclusion of the game he went straight to Southampton for Somerset's return game against Hampshire. Electing to bat Lionel started in fine form immediately opening up with some fine drives, pulls and cuts. He kept losing partners, and it was not until Robson arrived that he made a long partnership. At the close Somerset had reached 417 for seven with Lionel unbeaten on 251; his only chance was a simple one to Tom Soar when 141.

The following morning the pair took their partnership to 131 before Robson was run out; Lionel fell shortly afterwards for 292, having hit 44 boundaries in a stay of six and a half hours. Somerset went on to win by eight wickets. In two innings against Hampshire he had scored 439 runs for once out; his innings would remain the highest score by a Somerset batsman until it was broken by Harold Gimblett in 1948.

Lionel was then picked for the second Gentlemen-Players game of the season, at Lord's. The Gentlemen won by six wickets; Lionel started well in both innings but could only make 22 and 18.

It was not until the game against Middlesex at Taunton that he returned to his best form as he scored 35 and 63. Thanks to a second innings century by William Roe, Somerset held on to a creditable draw. The team played Sussex from August 6. In good weather and on an excellent wicket Sussex elected to bat, and stayed in the field for well over a day, finally dismissed for 559.

In reply Somerset soon lost Challen, but then the two Palairets came together and both batted magnificently for the rest of the day, adding 174 as the team closed on 181 for one; Lionel being the most aggressive as he closed on 109. The following morning the pair continued where they had left off, adding 249 for the second wicket until Lionel was out for 154. His innings lasted only two hours and 50 minutes, and included 26 fours. With the score at 348, Richard was out for a career best 156, his second and final century in first class cricket. The game ended in a draw with Somerset finishing on 476 for six at close.

Somerset narrowly held on for a draw against Kent, then looked forward to the game against the Australians at Taunton, from August 24. Sadly the game was ruined by weather with the third day being washed out. Batting first Somerset had reached 156 for five; Lionel made only six, before the weather curtailed play for the day. Overnight rain made the wicket difficult; Somerset closed for 219 then bowled the Australians out for 129, with Ernest Robson taking six for 22. However by the close Somerset had slumped to 49 for six, Lionel being bowled by McKibbin for a duck. Somerset at the close were 139 on with four wickets left.

The final county game at Taunton saw Surrey beaten by nine wickets, Lionel's 20 and 36 being useful. However the county slipped to eleventh in the championship winning only three of the 16 matches. The Championship was won by Yorkshire who were building a formidable team.

LCH playing forward

Before the season drew to a close, Lionel accepted an invitation to play for CI Thornton's eleven against the Australians at Scarborough, as part of the end of season festival. Opening the batting with Stanley Jackson, the pair put on 119 in 90 minutes with neither making a mistake; the stand eventually broken by George Giffen. Lionel had hit eight fours and the crowd cheered him off as he was dismissed, having made a fine 71. After the pair were separated Australia steadily took wickets and the innings closed for 294. In reply the Australians broke down badly in each innings as Bobby Peel took 12 for 96 in the match, the Australians going down by an innings and 38 runs.

Lionel again had a fine season scoring 1,362 runs at 41.27. This put him eighth in the national averages. *Wisden* noted that 'although he had a fine season and easily stood out as head and shoulders above his county colleagues he was not chosen to play for England during the summer'. Clearly playing for the Gentlemen was his opportunity to shine.

Lionel's first cricket of 1897 was in the county trial match; he could only make four. The first county game started on May 17 against Yorkshire at Taunton. Somerset having been made to follow on, Lionel began his second innings with some hard flowing drives. Opening with his younger brother the pair sent up 50 in 35 minutes. At 80, his younger brother fell to a fine catch by John Tunnicliffe at slip. The 100 was sent up after 80 minutes and immediately afterwards Lionel reached his fifty. Lionel fell to a good caught and bowled by Scofield Haigh for 79; at this point Somerset were making a fight of the game as they had reached 158 for three. Sadly though although Ernest Robson made 80 the innings fell away to 276 all out, and Yorkshire went on to win by five wickets.

The next match was not for three weeks against Middlesex at Lord's. Although the game was ruined by the weather Lionel made a fine 92 in two hours, his innings ended by a brilliant catch at the wicket by MacGregor. Lionel added 118 for the second wicket with his brother who made 56. Lionel's was described by the press as 'a brilliant innings'. The press noted that 'The Middlesex players showed off the new county cap for the first time'.

Travelling to Hove, Somerset lost an exciting match by one wicket. Setting Sussex only 101 to win in the fourth innings, with Somerset bowling well and supported by some smart catches, an unlikely win looked on the cards when the last pair came together (Frederick Parris and Fred Tate) and by some resolute cricket the pair held their nerves for an exciting finish. The game was finished by an upper cut for four by Parris off Robson. Lionel did little with the bat however.

After three winless opening games Somerset went to the Oval, to produce their best all-round display of cricket during the summer. By some consistent batting Somerset put up 349 in their first innings, Lionel making a quick 42, being second out at 65. Surrey made 249 with Tyler (six for 86) taking chief honours. Somerset again batted well reaching 274, with a hard-hit 88 from the captain Sam Woods. Lionel again was going well until a good ball from Walter Lees bowled him for 28. Facing 375 runs to win, Surrey again struggled against Tyler as he took seven for 77 and Somerset won by 224 runs. Sadly this form was not continued; Surrey would go onto finish second in the Championship.

Lionel missed the next three games, all lost; he returned for the game against Kent at Blackheath starting on July 15. Although he made two starts (16 and 32) the county was heavily beaten again, this time by 213 runs. The next game was at Bath as Somerset entertained the visiting Philadelphians. Sadly Lionel was bowled for a duck, by JB King the great American all-rounder. The game was badly affected by the weather and in reply to Somerset's 200, the Philadelphians could only progress to 171 for five.

Business then kept Lionel out of the next two games. When he returned at Taunton against Middlesex on August 2, the county had lost six county games in a row, most of them by heavy margins. Electing to bat Middlesex put together a good score of 363, with Andrew Stoddart making 109. In reply Lionel made a 'superior and stylish 72' the *Dundee Courier* reported, which included eleven fours. Although Middlesex were bowled for 190 in their second innings, Somerset then collapsed to 72 for eight, with defeat looking certain, but resolute defence by Fowler, Porch and Tyler meant the county held on for a draw.

Somerset's poor run continued as Sussex beat them by nine wickets at Taunton; the sequence was broken with a good win by 80 runs in the return with Kent. Lionel (with 16 and 2) had a poor match. The next game against Gloucestershire was badly affected by rain and ended in a draw.

Somerset then entertained Surrey and in completing the double over them denied Surrey the Championship. In a low-scoring game Somerset won by 66 runs. Lionel's poor form continued as he made none and 18. The last Championship match was again badly affected by rain with only the Hampshire innings completed and Somerset only just starting their reply.

Somerset again endured a poor season finishing eleventh; as in 1896 they won only three games. *Wisden* put Somerset's failures down to indifferent batting. Lionel topped the averages with 593 runs at 29.65 but he missed half the season to business. No one else averaged over 25 in the Championship. Tyler and particularly

Woods were finding it harder to come by wickets; the side was in desperate need of stronger bowling, though overall Wisden concluded that the bowling would have won more games if the batting had not been so frail. For Lionel it had been a poor season; apart from not scoring a century, he never played regularly and only played the odd non-county game. I think his poor season was partly down to lack of practice and not playing regularly.

Perhaps to keep fit, he played some football and in April 1898 was playing for Taunton Football Club, a forerunner to the current Taunton Town formed in 1947 and not connected to the original team. This season marks the last known football game by Lionel, when on April 19 Taunton played Yeovil Casuals in the Somerset Cup. Lionel, obviously past his best, was recorded by the press as 'missing a number of good chances'. Also playing with him were Ernest Robson and Beaumont Cranfield both Somerset county cricket players. Lionel did not appear in the replay; he could have thought it was time to finally hang up his boots. He also tried his hand at hockey, turning out for a game for Taunton against Bridgwater. With 200 in attendance the match ended in a 2-2 draw, with Lionel scoring the first for Taunton; this is the only known reference to him playing hockey.

It would appear he was at least keeping fit for the forthcoming season. He again played in the colts' match, which was titled L Palairet's eleven versus SMJ Woods' eleven, played at Taunton, on May 11 and 12. He made a good 57, the match though did not produce any potential new worthwhile county players. The prospects for the team looked bleak. The bowling was weak, with Woods and Nichols being virtually finished as effective bowlers. Tyler was still taking wickets but was having more off days and by 1900 virtually finished, as he was called for throwing by Jim Phillips. Robson was a useful all-rounder but had yet to make regular match-winning contributions. It was hoped George Gill and Bertie Cranfield, both having made their debuts the year before, would develop, if given more opportunities. The batting was also a problem. Lionel was playing less, and many of the old team were getting older or restricted from playing due to other commitments. One find from 1897 was Frank Phillips but his Army duties would limit his appearances for the county. Sam

Woods was still reliable as a batsman but his golden days as a fast bowler were well behind him. It was clear that the county needed new talent or would continue to struggle.

Against this backdrop of pessimism, the 1898 season opened at Bath against Yorkshire on May 16. The county were totally outplayed losing by 198 runs. A young Wilfred Rhodes, playing in his first championship match, took match figures of 13 for 45, and totally bamboozled the southern county. Lionel's first innings score of 26 was the highest in either Somerset innings; the team could only make 35 at their second attempt.

Without Lionel the team beat Oxford University late in May by 100 runs, Gill bowling quickly having match figures of 10 for 87, and Bertie Cranfield also bowling well. Hopes that the side would rejuvenate and have a good season were soon to be dashed. After a rain-affected draw with Middlesex, Somerset went to Eastbourne and thanks to a blistering 143 from Woods and 10 for 108 in the match by Tyler gained an easy victory by 108 runs after trailing by 69 runs on first innings. This early June victory would be the last of the season.

Lionel missed the next couple of county games; however he did play some minor games. On June 16 he scored 189 for Leighton against South Wiltshire, and the following day he added 70 playing for Leighton against Corinthians. At least he was keeping in practice and scoring some runs.

He then returned for Somerset against Lancashire at Taunton, starting on June 20. Lancashire were dismissed for 216 with only a brilliant 90 from JT Tyldesley holding the innings together. Batting first Lionel opened with a debutant John Daniell, whose debut innings was brief; after hitting a boundary he was caught off Willis Cuttell. Lionel was the only batsman to offer any resistance as in 95 minutes he scored a valuable 59. Though making a fine innings he was badly missed when 13. Somerset's innings closed for 135 and second time round Lancashire piled up 458, and went on to win by 260 runs. Daniell's appearance marked an association with the club that would last for over 40 years, as a player, captain and administrator.

After a defeat to Kent, the team travelled to the Oval to play Surrey. Having been made to follow on and going in second

Lionel with Sam Woods, Somerset captain from 1894 to 1906. The two men had no time for drawn matches

wicket down, Lionel played faultlessly for nearly three hours, and made 112, hitting 15 boundaries and with Woods (69) gave the team a chance of escaping with a draw. Surrey needed 153 in 105 minutes. Thanks to Bobby Abel and FC Holland, Surrey achieved their target with six minutes to spare. Lionel's bowling figures in the second innings were 17-5-51-0. Despite not taking a wicket, the local paper (*Taunton Courier*) praised him for bowling his lobs with great skill. This was a little odd as of the main bowlers Tyler only bowled six overs and Gill none during the second innings. Lionel had not bowled in the first innings.

Against Hampshire, Somerset after one innings each gained a lead of 115; at their second attempt Hampshire made 242 thanks largely to contributions from the lower order. Somerset though still needed only 128 runs for victory and would have expected to easily knock them off. Hampshire's Edward Tate had other ideas as he bowled a brilliant spell, taking eight for 51 and giving his county a well-earned nine run victory. Lionel had a poor match with the bat, contributing only 11 and 3.

Somerset's next game was against local rivals Gloucestershire at Bristol. Winning the toss, in good weather Gloucestershire batted all day, reaching 431 for five with centuries for Walter Troup and CL Townsend. The following morning the home team raised the score to 505 before being all out. Despite such a big total, and remembering what recently happened against Hampshire, Lionel was not called upon to bowl. Lionel entered the Somerset reply at the fall of the second wicket. He immediately started to attack the bowling. However at the other end wickets fell steadily and the team slipped to 87 for six but then Fowler came in. The pair added 125 in 90 minutes before Fowler was bowled for a good 39. Lionel who brought his own hundred up with the score at 200, had batted only one hour and 55 minutes. He continued to bat well and with Daniell added 91 for the ninth wicket. However Somerset could not avert the follow-on as they were eventually dismissed for 319. Lionel had battled for three and a half hours for an unbeaten 179 which included 29 fours; he had given two chances at 45 and 134; but despite this, it had been a brilliant innings. On his return to the pavilion the Bristol faithful 'heartily cheered his return'. Somerset went on to lose by an innings and seven runs. In the second innings restored as opener, Lionel was going well until one of WG's slows beat him for 37.

Going north to play Yorkshire at Scarborough Somerset were well beaten, but then crossing to Liverpool, made a better fight of it, leading by 17 runs on the first innings. This was largely down to a good opening stand of 84 between Lionel and HT Stanley. Lionel went on to 71 before being smartly caught. Sadly the second innings saw a breakdown in the batting and Lancashire easily won.

Returning to Taunton for the opening August game against Middlesex, Somerset would have hoped their fortunes would change. Winning the toss, in good weather before a crowd of 5,000, Somerset batted. From the first ball Lionel got after the Middlesex attack. His fifty came out of 70 in 57 minutes, and after 75 minutes he had made 76 of 103. He then quietened down as he was joined by Phillips who made 65. Having just reached his hundred, Lionel was dismissed by Hearne for 104, made out of 164. After this the innings folded and Somerset were bowled for 221 on a good pitch. Middlesex's first innings 354 was enough for a win by ten wickets.

Lionel's good form continued as he then hit 60 in the drawn game with Sussex. In the return with Kent at Taunton starting on August 11, Somerset found their batting form. In good weather again, Kent were dismissed for a poor 210. Lionel opened and immediately went on the attack; he hit his 50 out of 61 in 65 minutes. By the close he had made 73 of 108. The second day witnessed some heavy scoring. Lionel soon went in the morning having hit 88 of 141, including eleven fours with only one chance at seven. The press described the innings as 'beautiful'. The talking point on the day was a stand of 240 in two and a half hours by Sam Woods and Vernon Hill, who hit a tired Kent attack all over the place. Both made hundreds and Somerset closed on 503. Sadly though even with a day to go Kent easily batted out for a draw. Lionel, having a long bowl, took one for 47 off 21 overs.

After an innings defeat to Gloucestershire, Somerset played their final county game of the season against Surrey at Taunton. In good weather Somerset elected to bat. After the early loss of

Stanley, both Palairets were together and they soon mastered the bowling, adding 149 in only an hour and three quarters, before Richard fell for 50. Lionel went shortly afterwards for a brilliant century, his fourth of the season. With Roe also hitting a century the county amassed 457. Again, despite making Surrey follow on, Somerset were unable to make inroads in the Surrey's second innings.

The season finished with Somerset joint bottom with Leicestershire; this was the first time the county had suffered this (and it would not be the last). With the mix of good weather in August and some washouts earlier in the season, many games were drawn. Of the 16 games Somerset had drawn ten. Nottinghamshire drew 13 games out of sixteen, winning only one, yet were nearly mid table, showing the flaw of the method of deciding the Championship.

Wisden put down Somerset's failures in the season to 'faulty fielding and lack of penetration to bowl teams out twice'. This is borne out in many results when Somerset put themselves into a good position but let it slip. For Somerset Lionel had a brilliant season; in Championship games alone he scored 1,028 runs at 44.60. The problem was the bowling. Tyler took 83 wickets at 24.56 in the Championship but the next best was Robson with 38. Gill bowled well at times but was expensive and Cranfield was not called into the team all season.

The season for Lionel was not quite over yet; he was invited to play in the Scarborough festival which started on August 29. In the first match he played for the Gentlemen against the Players. After dismissing the Players for 126, Lionel opened with Lord Hawke. He would go on to score 54 out of 85. This would be the last time he played in this representative match. He would score 15 in the second innings as his team easily won by eight wickets. In the six games he played for the Gentlemen, he only scored 235 runs at 19.58, only once reaching fifty. It would seem that the authorities thought of him as not quite being up to Test level, and his appearances for representative matches statistics would seem to bear this out. However as work and family commitments were now starting to affect his frequency of appearances, I think he was not that concerned about playing at the highest level; his future refusal to play in representative games and turning down a chance to tour Australia would indicate it was not his main priority in life. Over time the authorities seemed to stop asking him to play.

He stayed on at Scarborough to play for CI Thornton's eleven against Yorkshire; the match was drawn and Lionel was bowled in each innings by Ted Wainwright (for 11 and 18). Despite this he had a fine season; in all matches he scored 1,126 runs at 41.70, and for most of the season scored consistently well. It appears Lionel then spent a short while in Scotland with a team from Wiltshire. He played a two day game for Fetteresso Castle against Stonehaven Thistle and took eight wickets in the match; despite this his team lost.

*LCH's natural batting
stance*

Chapter five
A new century and 1901

In November 1898 Lionel was elected onto the Somerset County Cricket Club committee. However just as the press were looking at the counties' prospects for the 1899 season, stating that Lionel would play as regularly as possible, he was struck down by appendicitis in late April. For its time this was a major operation; in the press it was well reported that he had had a serious operation. His friend, and fellow cricketer Gerald Fowler would succumb to this, as his appendix ruptured and he died of peritonitis in 1916, at 49.

For a while it was reported that Lionel would return in August, but in the end he missed all of the season. In his absence Somerset had a marginally better season winning two matches and finishing joint thirteenth. In his absence Charles Bernard, an opening batsman from the Bristol area who played his club cricket for the Bohemians, was tried and put together a number of useful innings. It was hoped that Somerset had found a new opening partner for Lionel. Sadly by 1901 having lost form he returned to club cricket, though he had the pleasure of hitting a century in his last match for the county.

On a brighter note, his brother Richard married in November; the best man was Plum Warner. It is ironic that over thirty years later, these two would be managers on the bodyline tour to Australia. Unlike Lionel who went to Devon for his honeymoon, Richard travelled around Europe.

The press was interested in Lionel's progress at the start of the new century; it was reported that he was fit and well. He also attended a number of the Somerset and Devon Staghounds meetings during the winter and spring. On May 12, the *Lancashire Evening Post* commented on the 'country looking forward to his presence again on the field and his masterful artistry of his batting, and how easily he scored his runs and how attractive and pleasing was his play for all crowds'.

He began his 1900 season with a couple of games for Taunton, first against Bridgwater; George Gill had him caught for a duck. Against Wellington a couple of days later, he made an attractive

72. Lionel made his eagerly awaited return to county cricket against Hampshire at Bath, on May 24. Somerset won by seven wickets. Lionel failed in each innings, the game being dominated by Ted Tyler who took 13 for 135 in the match and in the first innings hit a lusty 51.

After an innings defeat against Gloucestershire the side travelled to Lord's to play Middlesex, who won easily. In the second innings Lionel made his first notable innings of the season making 52. However the match will be remembered for Len Braund making his first Somerset appearance. Braund was a Surrey man who had been brought through the colts; he had made several centuries and taken some wickets for the second team. Despite making his debut in 1896 for the Surrey first team, he had been unable to hold a place down and his bowling had hardly been used. By the close of 1898 the Somerset committee had persuaded him to qualify for them as a professional.

He used his qualifying period well, playing for London County and other scratch sides and the odd non-Championship for Somerset. During this time he improved as a batsman and developed his leg spin, so that by the time he played against Middlesex he was already a noted all-rounder of immense ability. Sadly after the game with Middlesex, the authorities deemed that he was not qualified until the end of 1900. Had he been an amateur, this may have been overlooked (Ranjitsinjhi for a start was never qualified for Sussex when he first played – he didn't even reside in the county). Braund therefore had to go back to the London County and wait another year. Somerset badly needed him. Once qualified he would stay until 1920 and be a solid batsman, brilliant fielder and for a while a world-class all-rounder. He would play 23 Tests for England; more importantly for Somerset, he would form an excellent opening partnership with Lionel, by far the best since Hewett left in 1893.

Somerset's next game was against Sussex at Hove and thanks to 222 from Ranjitsinjhi the county was well beaten by ten wickets. Sam Woods hit a brilliant 148 in the first innings, but as so often in the second innings the batting broke down badly. Lionel was going well in the first innings making 45 but then was beaten by a good ball from Cyril Bland. Better luck followed at the Oval;

Somerset won easily by 171 runs. Lionel again contributed little, and to date had made only one innings of any note.

Then against Lancashire at Taunton starting on June 21, he made 59 and 30, top scoring for Somerset in both innings. Despite this most of his other colleagues struggled against Mold and Cuttell and the side was easily beaten by an innings. At Liverpool, Lionel narrowly avoided a pair by scoring nought and one. In the second innings Somerset were all out for 40 as Sharp and Briggs ran through the team; no-one made double figures and Somerset were again heavily beaten by an innings.

Lionel missed the next game with Kent due to work commitments. He returned to play Hampshire at Southampton, his form being the lowest of his career. Electing to bat the team slipped to 34 for two before Bernard joined Lionel. Shortly after Lionel gave a hard chance to the wicketkeeper when 28. After this his play and confidence increased. He reached his fifty out of 76 in 70 minutes. His hundred came up out of 154 in two hours and 10 minutes. The partnership continued and Bernard started scoring freely. The pair added 262 for the third wicket in three hours. Both were dismissed in the same over. Lionel batted three and a half hours, hitting 24 boundaries; he gave two difficult chances. Bernard fell for 122, his maiden first class hundred.

For a change Somerset did not let this position slip as Hampshire followed on having been dismissed for 218. Lionel's lobs yielded three for 46 as he dismissed two top order batsman. In the follow-on Hampshire made 279, but Somerset triumphed by an innings and six runs. Two developing bowlers Gill and Cranfield contributed well with the ball.

The Hampshire innings seemed to start Lionel's season as a batsman. In the next game he made a fluent 66. However having controlled most of the match, Somerset were beaten by one wicket, as Reginald Rice (who made an unbeaten 82) and last man Paish added 35 for the last wicket, to snatch a Gloucestershire win by one wicket. Lionel took two for 19 in the second innings and perhaps should have bowled more than his nine overs.

Len Braund, perhaps Lionel's greatest opening partner, a reliable and gifted all-rounder who played on until 1920

The team repeated the match with Gloucestershire, in the next game against Middlesex at Taunton. Somerset won the toss yet elected to bat on a wicket that was drying out under the hot sun. With play commencing at 3.15pm, the team were shot out for 89. Middlesex then posted 139 and gained a decisive advantage. Going in for the second innings Lionel and Bernard at last made a telling opening contribution. The pair knocked off the arrears in less than 40 minutes. The pair added 126 in an hour and 35 minutes, before Bernard was well caught for 72. Lionel then added 80 with Robson at a run a minute, with Robson making 50, batting brilliantly. Lionel fell at 243, having made 92 without a blemish, his chief hits being a six (off Jack Hearne) and 13 fours. After his dismissal the innings subsided to 327 all out. Middlesex were set a challenging total of 278. With the last pair requiring eight, Somerset still had a chance, but Trott made two lusty blows and the game was lost.

In the next game against Sussex at Taunton, which due to the weather was drawn, Lionel was denied another century, this time falling for 96, made in nearly two and half hours. Having lost the whole of the first day, his innings with 58 from Woods saved the team from probable defeat.

Against Kent at Taunton, Lionel scored at least fifty in an innings for the fifth successive match. In the second innings facing arrears of over 200, Lionel decided all-out attack was the best policy. After losing Robson at nine he was joined by Albert Lewis, a professional who was engaged to replace Nichols. Known as 'Talbot' he was a very useful batsman who over the next few seasons would develop his bowling, becoming a very useful member of the team. Lionel reached his fifty in 55 minutes, and the pair added 100 for the second wicket in 75 minutes before Lewis fell. Lionel fell at 130, having batted one and three quarter hours, giving only one chance off Bradley. Despite Gill and Tyler adding 135 for the ninth wicket, Somerset still went down by an innings.

After an innings defeat by Yorkshire, who were to replace Surrey as county champions and went through a 28-game season unbeaten, Somerset then started their last game of the season at Taunton against Surrey. Having lost the Championship, Surrey were having a bad season and were only mid-table. Having already beaten them heavily at the Oval, Somerset were confident of achieving the double.

Batting first Somerset owed their score of 221 to Lionel who made 83 in two hours and ten minutes, being fifth out at 135. With the wicket being very soft on top it was a fine innings, marred by only one chance off Lees when seven. When Surrey commenced their innings, Ted Tyler during his second over was no-balled for throwing by Jim Phillips. Woods took him off, and he only bowled one more ball in the match as he came back at the end of the innings to dismiss Tom Richardson and close the Surrey innings for 281.

This effectively finished Tyler as bowler, though with a remodelled action he did make a minor comeback in 1907, when the team was in disarray and really struggling for bowlers. Like several other cricketers of the time it was a sad way to end a career. Tyler had been one of the main reasons for Somerset gaining first-class status, and was the main bowler during the side's first decade in the Championship. Thanks to a brilliant hundred by Woods in the second innings and Cranfield's match figures of 12 for 118, Somerset duly completed the double over Surrey, winning a close match by 26 runs.

Somerset had finished the season with four wins and were placed eleventh in the Championship. Prospects for the team appeared to be good. New bowlers were coming to the fore in Cranfield and Gill, Robson had a good all round season, Albert Lewis promised to be a useful addition and hopes were high for Bernard; and Somerset could look forward to Braund being able to play next season.

Lionel was back in the side, playing in most of the games, and after a poor start still managed to score 947 runs at 35.07. He and Woods still formed the main engine room of the side. Hopes then were high for 1901 and continued improvement.

In the winter, Lionel attended a number of foxhound meetings. His first cricket game of the 1901 season took place at Taunton on April 27, when he played in the first match for the Somerset Stragglers against Taunton. The Stragglers were a team founded by Rev EP Spurway, who had played twice for the county. The amateur club played their home grounds at Taunton until the 1970s, and still exists. The team often had many of the county's amateurs playing for them; the club's heyday was in the 1930s when over 70 fixtures were arranged in a season.

For this first game a number of the top Somerset amateurs played, and attracted over 1,000 spectators. Batting first the Stragglers ran up 228 with Lionel top scoring with a faultless 123. The Taunton attack included Braund, Robson and Tyler, all county men. Taunton knocked the runs off easily with Braund replying with an unbeaten hundred. Lionel also took the first wicket for the Stragglers when he dismissed Sloman.

This would be the start of his greatest season in county cricket and by the end of the season, the press would state he should be an automatic choice for England; he had the reputation of being one of England's current greatest batsman.

The county season started on Monday, May 13 at Taunton against Yorkshire. According to the *Taunton Courier* 'the weather was dull and rather cool at noon'. The local press also commented that the home team had a strong eleven. After Somerset won the toss Lionel and Lewis opened in front of a small crowd. A big plus for the county was that Braund was now fully qualified to play and he would lift the Somerset batting and bowling.

Lionel settled immediately and started to find the boundary with regularity. At 55 he was dropped at mid-off, the unlucky bowler being George Hirst. At lunch the score stood at 155 for one with Lionel unbeaten on 101. With Lewis he had added 103 for the first wicket. After the interval Lionel soon fell, bowled by Hirst for 103. He had batted two hours ten minutes, had hit a six into the churchyard (off Rhodes), and added 15 fours.

After this, by consistent batting Somerset totalled 349. Yorkshire headed this by 42, which was to prove decisive. At their second attempt Somerset batted well for 281, with Sam Woods making a fine 90; Lionel had been going well until he hit a return catch back to Rhodes for 38. So in the final innings Yorkshire required 240; at 119 for six victory looked certain to go to Somerset, but Wainwright and Lord Hawke both made fifties. With the last pair needing two runs to win they just got home amidst great excitement. For the losers Braund made a great effort for his side, finishing with match figures of 10 for 268. Somerset had fought well and given the champions a good game; the return later in the summer would be even more dramatic.

After such a good performance in the first game, Somerset would have travelled in good spirits to play Middlesex at Lord's. However the team was badly beaten. Plum Warner carried his bat for 197 in the second innings, and Somerset were set 464 in well under a day. Although Lionel made 55 of the first 82 in 'charming style' (according to the *Taunton Courier*), the team were then already four down. Apart from Woods (83) no one else lasted long and the innings closed for 205, Somerset losing by 258 runs.

Somerset followed this with an even heavier defeat at Hove to Sussex, by an innings and 39 runs; Ranjitsinjhi made 133 for the home team. Lionel top scored in the second innings with a fluent 52, but he seemed to become over-confident and was stumped just after reaching his half-century.

A third successive heavy defeat came against Surrey at the Oval by 204 runs. Again the batting badly let Somerset down; Lionel's first innings of 47 was the highest score in either of Somerset's innings. After four Championship games the team had lost them all and was bottom (with Derbyshire) of the table. Hopes of a good season had already evaporated.

The next game was a friendly against Oxford University at The Parks. For a change Lionel travelled to play his old university. Somerset took a weak team, though making his debut was Henry Martyn, who was at Oxford University. Born in Devon, Martyn was a brilliant wicket-keeper who stood up to almost any bowler, slow or fast. He was to render useful service to Somerset as an amateur, though after 1906 he dropped out of cricket due to work commitments; this was particularly sad as he was developing into a fine batsman. His finest hour was his unbeaten 130 against the Australians in 1905. Like Lionel he turned down the chance to tour Australia in 1903-04.

At Oxford, Somerset won the toss and batted. Lionel went in at the fall of the second wicket at 39. He hit a fine 73, but the county could only post 173. In reply Cranfield and Gill shot out the students for only 81. By the close of play Somerset reached 94 for one with Lionel on 67. He was out early the following

morning for 72, made out of 99. Ernest Robson stole the show
with a brilliant unbeaten 163, with five sixes out of the ground
and 19 fours. Despite a brilliant hundred from EW Dillon,
Somerset won by the end of the second day by 233 runs, a much
needed win.

The next game was at Taunton against the visiting South
Africans, who although were not quite ready for Test matches
were granted a first-class tour after a 1894 tour not first class.
Somerset were reported in the press as having a 'weak team'.
Again after winning the toss, Lionel opened with another
new promising undergraduate player Peter Johnson, who was
qualifying for the county. Johnson was studying at Cambridge
and would gain his blue that year. He was a tall stylish batsman
who would play when he could for Somerset until 1927, scoring
over 10,000 runs and hitting 17 centuries for the club. It appeared
that Somerset were finding new younger players who would
serve them well over the coming years.

Winning the toss Lionel opened with Johnson, and the pair
added 50 before Johnson fell to JJ Kotze for 11. Lionel was
second to go at 114, having made 72. In three hours and forty
minutes, Somerset ran up 313. Somerset bowled the visitors by
124 at the close of play, George Gill, bowling fast, bowled all
five of his victims for 24. Against tradition Somerset did not
enforce the follow-on. Lionel with Johnson this time added 83
in 45 minutes before Lionel was caught for 52. The onslaught
continued and Somerset declared on 440 for nine, made in just
four hours and 15 minutes. Lewis made his first hundred for the
county, but it was Gill's 85 that caused the most excitement.
After reaching 50, he then hit EA Halliwell onto the shilling
stand and then into the pavilion. GA Rowe then was brought on
at the pavilion end; in one over Gill hit him on to the top of the
pavilion, then into the shilling stand and twice onto the pavilion
rails; the crowd, though not large, greeted these hits with great
enthusiasm. Set an impossible task of 630 the South Africans
went on to lose by 341 runs. At least these last two games meant
many of the players were now in form. At the end of the tour the
South African captain Murray Bisset was asked who was the best
batsman they played against, and he stated without doubt Lionel

Palairet. A fine compliment from Bisset, but it just underlines the impression Lionel was leaving on players within the first-class game.

The team would have had high hopes in Somerset's next game, which was at home to Worcestershire at Bath. Worcestershire were new to the Championship as they were only admitted in 1899. Worcestershire's first two seasons had seen them struggle. This year seemed no better as they had won only once and lost seven games in the Championship, many heavily. The start of the game was delayed due to rain; Worcestershire struggled on a difficult wicket and made 157. Then opening with Bernard, Lionel was bowled first ball by George Wilson, a fast right-arm bowler. The innings closed with a deficit of 59, although Worcestershire's second innings amounted to only 110, with Cranfield taking seven for 48. Somerset were only set 172; however the wicket was still difficult, Lionel fell for 17 and Somerset lost by 26 runs.

Staying at Bath for the visit of Lancashire, in brilliant hot weather Somerset won the toss and elected to bat. Lionel hit three fours in Mold's first over. However when 21 Lionel was dropped at cover slip by John Holland; this chance would cost Lancashire dearly. Lionel sent up his fifty out of 64 in 40 minutes. He and Braund continued scoring rapidly, sending up the hundred in less than an hour; Mold, the reliable fast bowler, coming in for some heavy treatment. Lionel reached his century in an hour and 50 minutes, when the opening partnership had increased to 166. Lionel had given another chance at 61 but otherwise he played a fine innings. At lunch Lionel was unbeaten on 114 with the opening stand worth 188.

After the resumption the opening partnership continued until 225, when Braund was bowled by part-time bowler Albert Ward for 82. The *Manchester Courier* said 'Palairet's strokes were so clean, so sharp, and so crisp, that his cricket all-round the wicket commanded great attention'. Lionel continued scoring quickly and reached his own 150 in two and three quarter hours. He eventually was second out at 298, after three and a quarter hours, hitting 28 fours. Somerset batted well into the second day and amassed an imposing 561; a demoralised Lancashire were easily beaten by an innings and 117 runs, and this emphatic win was

Somerset's first Championship victory of the season.

Somerset immediately travelled to Bristol to face Gloucestershire. Played on a soft wicket due to recent rain, the game started just after noon. Woods having won the toss sent in Lionel and Braund. Lionel was the only one who settled on the wicket; he made many fine drives and the total reached 50 at a run a minute. Lionel brought his own fifty up in an hour and a quarter. He was soon out for 61; he gave only one chance just before he was dismissed. After his departure at 93 for three, the innings fell away and the side made only 197.

This total was more than enough for a substantial lead of 79, as Cranfield and Gill ran through Gloucestershire. Going in a second time with the wicket still not easy, Lionel carried on where he had left off. The press noted that his innings was marked with some 'high hard drives'. Again he was the only player to master the conditions; he posted his second fifty of the match in one and three quarter hours. He eventually fell for 82 in two and a quarter hours, his chief hits being a six and eleven fours. Again after his dismissal the innings fell apart, the last six wickets falling for 55. However Gloucestershire, set 268 on a difficult wicket, thanks to Braund (seven for 70) never had the remotest chance, being all out for 139. Lionel was the only player in the match to score fifty, Wrathall's 39 for Gloucestershire being the next best.

Somerset then had a week's break, preparing for the northern tour to play Lancashire and Yorkshire. These two games would be talked about for years to come, but both for different reasons. The first game against Lancashire was eagerly awaited; Lancashire wanted revenge for their innings defeat only a fortnight earlier. The first day's play though was overshadowed by the umpire Jim Phillips. The *Manchester Courier* takes up the story:

'The spectators at Old Trafford yesterday had plenty of entertainment. The match promised to be interesting before a ball was bowled, but it proved sensational, within a few minutes of the start, and altogether the events of the day may be described as of history making character so far as county cricket is concerned. The sensation of the day was the attitude of Phillips, the umpire towards Mold. Winning the toss,

Somerset commenced their innings with Palairet and Braund to the bowling of Hallows and Mold. Each bowler sent down an over and it was not until Hallows completed his second over that the sensations commenced.

'His first ball passed safely, but Phillips then challenged the second and third deliveries, when putting up his hand shouted 'no-ball' to each. Instantly there were loud shouts of disapproval from the crowd (about 1,000 being present at the ground). But this did not deter Phillips who kept calling Mold for throwing. The over eventually amounted to eleven balls, five being called no-ball.

'At the other end there was total silence from Richardson, Hallows then bowled his third over and Mold was then replaced by Webb, this change did not meet the approval of the Old Trafford crowd who continued to shout and boo. The crowd appeared to regard it as a capitulation to the decisions of Phillips and they took vehement notice of the fact.

'MacLaren, though had a card up his sleeve. If Phillips at square-leg could discern what Richardson at the bowler's end could not, it was only fair that both should have the judgement accordingly. As a result Mold replaced Hallows. The crowd cheered this action. Now came the test. Phillips could not watch the feet as well as the action of the bowler and Phillips apparently was content with watching the style of the bowler (Mold).

'The first ball went unchallenged, but on the second he raised his arm at square leg and called no-ball. Phillips repeated the call for the fourth and fifth deliveries. There were three no balls in this over. The crowd now were now barracking Phillips, calling him some uncomplimentary names. Phillips ignored this and continued to call no balls. Meanwhile Palairet and Braund batted on and showed little disturbance to their batting amidst what was going on around them.

'In Mold's next over Phillips called him four times for no balling. Only one was called in each of Mold's next two overs. In his seventh none were called and Mold had Palairet caught at mid-wicket and clean bowled Jupp two deliveries later. The eighth and ninth each had one no-ball called. In the tenth another no-ball was called, this made the total 18 of which three were scored off.'

After this Phillips did not call Mold again during the innings or the match; Webb was called for one no-ball by Richardson for overstepping. The game continued amidst a lot of calling by the spectators aimed at Phillips. The day's cricket, now taking second to the events, continued and by the close Lancashire had reached 275 for three in reply to Somerset's 253, Tyldesley still being in on 168.

The events were reported in great detail by the press and the following morning several thousand turned up to see if they would see a repeat of the first day. What it did do was to get the interest of Mitchell and Kenyon who were a film company based in Blackburn. The company were early pioneers of commercial motion pictures. At the time they were noted for their dramatisation of the Boer War. The company also would film various sporting events and as a result of the first day events, they appeared at the ground to film proceedings (possibly with the hope of a recording Arthur Mold being called for throwing again).

As a result, the teams were filmed as they left the field at lunch, Lancashire having been dismissed for 354 and Somerset going in one wicket down. Lionel is shown leaving the field talking to Archie MacLaren. He appears, 15 seconds into the video (this can be seen on *YouTube*) and is in shot for 12 seconds. He is wearing his Harlequin cap, he is tall, very slim and walks with an air of authority and he even gazes at the camera as he leaves the field. What a pity the cameramen did not film some of Lionel's batting; furthermore it is almost certainly the only live film we have of him. Somerset were dismissed by tea and lost the match by ten wickets. Lionel made 29 and 23. More importantly it virtually finished Mold's career.

If this match caused a stir in the cricket world, the following game with Yorkshire at Headingley matched it, but this time for the play. The game started just after noon to a good crowd of nearly 8,000. Winning the toss, the now regular opening pair of Lionel and Braund commenced the innings; both were out for nought. After barely an hour and a half the side was dismissed for 87, with Woods making over half (46).

By the close of play Yorkshire were all out for 325, taking a lead of 238 runs into the second day. At this point the Yorkshire Post commented that 'Yorkshire have another comfortable victory in prospect'. In the evening the Somerset team were entertained by the Mayor of Leeds. It is alleged he promised that he would give the club £100, if Somerset could beat Yorkshire. Woods accepted the bet. However many of the team were planning to travel back to Somerset by the end of the second day, with the game poised in favour of Yorkshire. Apart from Woods no-one expected Somerset to win.

Somerset commenced their second innings at 11.30am in hot sunny conditions, with only about 2,000 present. From the start Lionel and Braund got after the Yorkshire bowling. The pair soon sent the fifty up in 35 minutes. Lionel was the first to raise his fifty in just over the hour; Braund soon followed ten minutes later but already he had been dropped twice. By lunchtime the score had been raised to 222 in two hours and 20 minutes when Braund was bowled by Haigh for 107; Lionel went in unbeaten on 112. The Yorkshire team were unhappy as they thought they had Braund caught at short slip by Tunnicliffe when he had made 55; Braund stood his ground and as no umpire could see if a fair catch had been made, the umpires ruled in Braund's favour. Those who saw the catch said it was a fair catch.

Lionel continued and was almost caught at point when 135 off Rhodes. He continued in fine form until on 173 he gave a simple return catch to John Brown, the score now 341 for three. His innings had lasted three hours and 40 minutes and he had hit 28 fours. The hitting continued; Frank Phillips made 122 and Woods hit 66, as Somerset closed day two on 549 for five, the most runs the team has ever hit in a day. The following day this total was raised to 630 before Somerset were all out. Poor George Hirst had endured the worst day and a half of his bowling career as he took one for 189 off 37 overs.

With only a draw to play for Yorkshire reached 57 for one before Cranfield and Braund ran through them for 113. Yorkshire actually lost their last six wickets for only 14. Somerset had won an incredible game by 279 runs, and even today this must be the greatest victory in the club's history. Yorkshire had not lost a Championship match since 1899 and this was the 48th game they had played since. On the conclusion of the team's victory the Yorkshire crowd appreciated the fight-back of Somerset, surrounding the pavilion and applauding. After cries of 'speech', Sammy Woods came out smiling and waved, Braund and Lionel also had to make an appearance to the excited crowd. Sammy never got his money from the mayor. On the team's return a large crowd gathered at the train station in Taunton to welcome the team home; the players must have felt like heroes.

After the excitement of Headingley, the team then travelled to Portsmouth in Hampshire the following week. After Hampshire made a good total of 372, Lionel and Braund commenced the innings and hit well as the day closed with Somerset on 89 without loss, Lionel having just reached his fifty. The following morning the pair continued in fine form. The opening partnership reached 196 when Lionel was bowled for 96; he had batted only two hours and five minutes, having hit nine fours and eight threes, in a delightful innings. Braund went for 111; a brilliant start was wasted as the team collapsed to 296, thereby trailing by 76 runs. Hampshire declared their innings, setting Somerset 276 to win. Lionel again batted well making a solid 64, but he found little support and Somerset crashed to 173 all out, to lose by 103 runs.

Lionel then missed a narrow defeat to Kent but returned to against Middlesex at Taunton. On a good wicket Somerset dismissed Middlesex for an acceptable 265; by the close Somerset had reached 103 for two with Lionel unbeaten on 52 and going well. The following morning he continued in the same form, until he had made 92 when he was caught at deep mid-off trying a huge drive. He had batted two hours and 55 minutes; among his hits were a six (off Richard More) and ten fours. Somerset went on to a first innings lead of 109; however they could not bowl Middlesex out a second time, and Middlesex easily saved the game. Lionel did help himself to an unbeaten 35 in the second innings as the match petered out.

The visit of Sussex immediately followed. Lionel's great form continued. Sussex batted on a good wicket and struggled to 236, despite George Brann making a century. By the close Lionel and Lewis had already made an unbeaten 158 for the first wicket with Lionel going in on 73. The following morning the partnership was raised to 258 when Lewis was caught for 120. Lionel then added 104 with Braund before he was out for an excellent 194; he had batted four hours ten minutes and hit 28 fours. Somerset were able to declare on 560 for eight. Somerset had just over a day to bowl Sussex out; however after an opening stand of 174 by Joe Vine and Ranjitsinjhi, Sussex batted the rest of the day without losing another wicket; they closed on 466 for one, Ranjitsinjhi making 285 and CB Fry 119 as the pair added an unbroken 292.

An innings defeat followed to Kent, although after Kent closed on the first day at 435 for four it rained and made the wicket treacherous; 26 wickets fell on the second day for only 181 runs, with Colin Blythe and John Mason bowling unchanged in each innings.

It was then back to Taunton and happily better weather for the visit of Surrey. Winning the toss Lionel and Braund started the Somerset innings. Both began shakily, snicking balls through the slips. Despite this both soon settled and scored freely. After half an hour fifty went up. After 55 minutes of play Lionel sent up his fifty. The opening stand was broken after an hour and a half, with Braund going for 44. With the score at only 149, Lionel reached a brilliant hundred. At lunch the score was 161 for one, Lionel having scored a fifth century of the season and all of them before lunch; an unrivalled feat in one season. In two of them he was not out overnight and added at least a hundred in the session. Lionel added 111 for the second wicket with Lewis (113), before he finally fell to William Brockwell for 140; his innings lasting two hours and fifty minutes, he had scored 19 boundaries. Somerset eventually posted 438, but solid batting in each innings by Bobby Abel and Tom Hayward ensured a draw for Surrey, Lionel adding 44 to his first innings century.

Lionel had a quiet time in the last two county games at Taunton; Somerset were heavily beaten by Hampshire and finishing the season against Gloucestershire the county beat their western rivals by 75 runs. There were centuries from Braund and Bernard.

Lionel finished the season with 1,906 runs at 57.75, hitting five centuries and eleven fifties. Other players had fine seasons, both Woods and Braund scored over a thousand runs and Cranfield took over 100 wickets. In all games Braund became the first Somerset player to do the double of 1,000 runs and 100 wickets; soon he would become an England player. Lewis also scored over 800 runs with three centuries, and Gill and Robson also had decent seasons.

Despite some fine personal achievements, Somerset actually slipped to joint twelfth in the Championship; as in 1900 they only won four games. This is a surprise considering the achievements of Lionel, Braund and Cranfield. The main problem with the team was bowling opponents out twice; generally, if Cranfield and Braund failed with the ball, the team did not win. In low scoring games if the major players failed, there did not seem to be enough depth in batting; a number of winnable games were lost as a result. Despite this there had been some memorable batting performances, with some big partnerships, with Lionel at the heart of many.

Of the regular players in 1901, Lionel was third to Sussex's Fry and Ranjitsinjhi in the national batting averages. The press were full of praises for his batting, and it also seemed a certainty that had there been a Test series he would have made his debut for England. With the Australians visiting in 1902, Lionel's name was pencilled in by many correspondents.

Chapter six
1902 and one more good season

After an entertaining season (though disappointing from the team's perspective), Somerset held its annual general meeting at the London Hotel in Taunton. Gerald Fowler, the honorary treasurer since 1896, yet again announced losses. It was agreed the club guarantors would pay for the shortfall. A club guarantor was a wealthy individual (there were about 30 to 40) who agreed to share any losses made by the club (which it often did) and they would pick up the shortfall; sometimes an element was made up by fund-raising and fetes around the county.

The club praised Lionel's and Len Braund's fine performances; Lionel was also elected as a Vice-President of Somerset. The meeting also agreed that it might take more games away from Taunton as games at Bath were well supported; as it turned out this would not happen for a number of years, other than at Weston super Mare just before the Great War.

In February it was mentioned again that Lionel was a possible candidate for the forthcoming series against Australia. The summer of 1902 would be very wet; however it did not seem to bother the great batsman Victor Trumper who was to score 2,570 runs at 48.49 including 12 centuries. The *Western Times* added: 'With the additions of Henry Martyn and Peter Johnson, the outlook for Somerset this year looks most promising.'

The season began well for Lionel with an innings of 85, as he guested for the Somerset Stragglers against Taunton, Somerset professional Lewis making a hundred for Taunton. It seemed Lionel might carry on where he left off. Sadly after making a useful 34 in the opening game against Oxford University, Lionel was to make a run of low scores. The first county game was won in exciting fashion by one wicket as fine fifties from Lewis, Robson and a match-winning unbeaten 88 from Sam Woods brought off a fine win at Lord's against Middlesex. Lionel made 27 and three, falling in each innings to Albert Trott.

Although having made a poor start to the season, he was included in the MCC side to play the Australians at Lord's starting on May 26, his only first-class game for the club. Clearly he was still in the plans of the selectors. With a strong batting line up he was batting with CB Fry, Ranjitsinhji, Len Braund, Plum Warner and the evergreen captain WG Grace.

In good weather Grace won the toss and elected to bat. Fry and Lionel opened for the MCC. Since it had rained the day before, both openers decided to force the pace from the off (the players were unsure whether the pitch would deteriorate in the sun). Hitting well the fifty was posted in less than half an hour. Luck was on the openers' side as Fry was badly missed on eight and Lionel was regularly beaten. The pair added 79 in 53 minutes before Fry fell lbw to Howell having made 36. Lionel was bowled at the same score by one of Trumper's medium pacers for 39. The innings closed for 240 which was headed by the visitors who made 271, thanks largely to a brilliant 105 from Trumper in only two hours.

Going in a second time, Fry and Lionel opened with a stand of 43; wickets fell regularly and Lionel watching from the other end played a cautious innings. At 105, having made 44, he was bowled by a shooter from Ernest Jones the Australian fast bowler. Afterwards with some steady batting the MCC declared on 280 for eight. Trumper made 86 in the second innings as the Australians fell 33 short of their target when time ran out. Lionel, though still without a major innings, had at least acquitted himself well.

In Somerset's next game the weather ruined a possible victory as with six wickets left Somerset required another 78 runs to win. Lionel with 19 and 31 was still looking for a major score.

Thanks largely to the bowling of Cranfield, Braund and Gill, Somerset registered their second win of the season at Bath, with a ten wicket victory over Hampshire, Lionel making a good 36 but falling again when set. He again failed in defeats to Gloucestershire and Yorkshire. The return match with Yorkshire at Sheffield provided another surprising win. On a difficult wicket Somerset won by 34 runs, thanks largely to Braund who had match figures of 15 for 71. Lionel made 25 and 24, vital contributions in a low scoring game. For the second successive year this was Yorkshire's only defeat in the Championship.

By the time he travelled to Worcester, he had played 14 innings without a fifty. As Somerset trailed by 59 on the first innings, Lionel went out with Braund. Lionel had made only two in the first innings. The pair hit up 48 before lunch, and added 57 in 45 minutes before Braund was dismissed. The wicket having had overnight rain was now crusty on top and was becoming harder to bat on. Lionel played excellent cricket but could not find any support as wickets started to tumble. He eventually fell for 82, seventh out at 156. He was at the wicket two hours and five minutes. The side eventually set Worcestershire 102 in 80 minutes, but the difficult wicket meant they closed on 51 for six. At least Lionel had scored his first fifty and in good style.

After a virtual washout of the second test, Australia beat England at Sheffield by 143 runs. Although he was not to know it at the time, Lionel would be drafted in for CB Fry, despite the fact that he was fairly out of form. While England were losing, Lionel was making nought and 13, in a three wicket loss to Gloucestershire. He did however take two for 55 and three for 28, with his now sparingly used lobs. Further misery for Somerset and Lionel continued, as they went down by five wickets to Hampshire at Portsmouth, Lionel making 40 and one. His bowling was put to use again as he took three for 50 in Hampshire's first innings.

Somerset then awaited the Australians at Taunton on July 17, another chance for Lionel to impress against the tourists. After Somerset won the toss Lionel and Braund opened the innings in cloudy weather, although it was soon to brighten after a brief shower and remain fine for the rest of the day. From the off both openers went after the bowling. The pair brought up fifty after only 45 minutes. After 70 minutes and with the score 88, Lionel was caught at the second attempt by Syd Gregory for 44; Somerset were eventually dismissed for a reasonable 274. Thanks to Reggie Duff (183), Australia gained a first innings lead of 74.

Starting the second innings at 3.40pm, Lionel started by hitting three fours off Jones in the first over. Jones almost grazed Braund's head with a short ball; this prompted Braund to protest to the umpire about careless and dangerous bowling (things have changed!). Lionel continued with some fine polished drives and cuts. At 54, Braund was bowled by Jones having made only six of the partnership and never looking comfortable. Lionel soon brought his fifty up in only 40 minutes. He slowed afterwards, mainly because of wickets falling at the other end, but his 90 out of 141 for four was made in two hours and ten minutes with 15 fours; he gave no chance. It is almost certain that this innings was responsible for his call-up to the Fourth Test team. Somerset afterwards rallied and eventually reached 315, sadly though rain came shortly after the Australians commenced their second innings.

After the defeat at Sheffield, with the Fourth Test starting the following week at Manchester, England made four changes. Out went CB Fry, George Hirst, Gilbert Jessop and Sydney Barnes. In came Ranjitsinjhi, Bill Lockwood (Surrey), Fred Tate (Sussex) and Lionel. Hirst ended up being twelfth man. Both Lockwood and Tate (the first to reach a hundred wickets in the season) were having fine seasons, with Ranjitsinjhi being recalled after missing the last Test. The committee choosing the team at Manchester consisted of Lord Hawke, Gregor MacGregor, HW Bainbridge, FS Jackson and AG Steel. Newspapers made little of Lionel's inclusion other than it was his first game and his innings of 90 had impressed the selectors; the newspapers agreed with his inclusion commenting on his graceful batting. Lionel had made only two fifties in the summer to date as it was nearly the end of July, so he was perhaps fortunate to have been chosen.

Australia won an important toss, electing to bat, on a dead and lifeless pitch. As a result Trumper and Duff opened with a sterling partnership of 135 before the stand was broken by Lockwood. Trumper went on to score 104 in only 115 minutes. As the day progressed the sun started to dry the wicket out, the England bowlers started getting more purchase on the ball and it became increasingly harder to make runs.

Although Clem Hill and Joe Darling made fifties, after such a good start the Australians were restricted to 299 made in four and a quarter hours. Bill Lockwood's return of six for 48 being particularly excellent. Lionel caught Hopkins at long-on off Lockwood. However by now the wicket was drying rapidly and it was expected that England would struggle to make runs from the outset.

At 5.15pm, Lionel and Bobby Abel strode to the wicket to face the opening Australian bowlers Hugh Trumble and John Saunders. With a close set field the pair were immediately in trouble, the ball popping and spitting from the turf; even survival looked a daunting prospect. Both openers went in the same over, Abel to a poor shot caught in the slips, then a run later Monty Noble caught Lionel smartly running in from point, his first Test innings ending for six (at 13 for two). By the close of play England had slumped to 70 for five.

Dry and fine weather on the second day made the wicket a lot easier. The following morning Jackson (128) and Braund (65) added 141 for the sixth wicket. England eventually closing for 262, only 37 runs in arrears. Going in a second time the Australians struggled from the first ball closing on 85 for eight, Lockwood again being the most difficult bowler to play. Australia were now only 122 runs on with two wickets left.

On the third morning the innings was wrapped up with an addition of one run, Lockwood (five for 28) again being England's best bowler, Lionel caught Darling off Rhodes, his second and last catch in Test cricket. At 12.40, Archie MacLaren replaced

Lionel's first Test innings, going out to bat with little Bobby Abel at Manchester in 1902

Abel and went out to open with Lionel, with only 124 required to level the series. Both started their innings cautiously and quite out of character, both sensing the need to play responsibly. Early in his innings Lionel was nearly caught by Gregory at short leg; despite this the pair survived the 50 minutes until lunch taking the score to 36. It was also apparent the wicket was become more treacherous.

After the interval things seemed to be picking up; the first two overs produced eight runs. Then from the last ball of the third over Lionel played late to Saunders and was bowled off stump for 17. Although wickets fell steadily England reached 107 for five and victory seemed assured. However Trumble got to work and Tate came to the wicket, last man in, with rain beginning to fall and England still needing another eight. As he got to the wicket amidst great excitement the umpires took the players off for rain.

At 4.45pm, Tate and Rhodes resumed for England after a delay of 40 minutes. After adding four, Saunders bowled Tate with a shooter and the game and Ashes went to Australia by only three runs. Poor Fred Tate was blamed and never played again; he had dropped a vital catch earlier, and many critics think he should not have played anyway. Fred though was having a fine season and was in the side on merit and unfairly criticised as the batting had let England down; his son Maurice would later be a leading all-rounder for Sussex and England. Lionel hardly had a great match, but both times when he batted the wicket was very difficult; he played no worse than other more experienced Test colleagues.

Lionel then went back to Somerset and continued his miserable summer making six and one as Somerset lost by an innings. He did far better in the next game at Taunton taking 42 and 25 off Middlesex as Somerset won by seven wickets, Lionel's two for 27 in the first innings also providing some useful support. He followed this with 28 in his only innings in the drawn game with Sussex.

On August 10, the England team was announced in the newspapers for the final Test at the Oval. Lionel was again chosen. The selectors made a number of changes; out went Abel, Ranjitsinhji and Tate, replaced by Tom Hayward (Surrey), Gilbert

Jessop (Gloucestershire) and George Hirst. The press generally reported that Lionel deserved to keep his place in the team.

Australia won the toss and thanks to some consistent batting, kept in England in the field all day making 324. Overnight it again rained heavily which would make the uncovered pitch difficult. In poor light MacLaren and Lionel opened the innings. After six overs MacLaren appealed to the umpires and the players came in. However with the sun creeping through, the break of 40 minutes affected the wicket further.

On resumption the wicket started playing tricks immediately with both openers finding it difficult. MacLaren fell first but Lionel soon followed bowled by Trumble for 20; this was to be his highest Test score. The innings fell away badly closing on 183, a deficit of 141 runs. With the wicket now difficult Australia cut an even poorer effort as they could only make 121, Lockwood with five for 45 being England's best bowler, yet again. This meant England had nearly a full day to make an improbable 263.

The overnight rain meant the wicket was soft and difficult. The innings started disastrously, Lionel, third out at ten, made only six, bowled by a vicious turning ball from the leg by Trumble. Half the side were gone for 48, and the 263 required looked a long way off. Amazingly England were to win one of the best and closest Test matches in history. Jackson made 49, but it was a hundred in 75 minutes by Gilbert Jessop that set the game up. Hirst made an unbeaten fifty and it was left to him and Rhodes to add 15 runs for the last wicket to pinch a dramatic victory; this match would be talked about for years by those fortunate enough to have witnessed Jessop's fine innings.

This brought Lionel's Test career to a close. His 49 runs at 12.25 per innings is not much to show; however he played in two great Test matches. All of his innings were on difficult wickets and no one else coped any better; it was not until the wicket played easier that his teammates scored runs.

Lionel then returned for Somerset's next match at Taunton against Kent. In a start delayed by rain, Kent foolishly elected to bat on a soft wicket; the Somerset bowlers shot out the visitors for only 66. By the close Somerset had progressed to 45 for two with Lionel unbeaten on 15. The second day saw an improvement in the wicket, Lionel and Frank Phillips adding 91 for the third wicket. All the other batsman struggled against Blythe and Mason who were still receiving a fair amount of help from the pitch. Lionel was last out at 189, having batted three hours and 35 minutes in making his 89. He batted in a class above his colleagues, combining sound defence with aggressive hitting when the opportunity came.

With the wicket easing Kent made 356 in the second innings, setting Somerset 234 to win. Somerset slipped to 99 for four and the result was in doubt. Lionel was still there and with some support the total reached 166 for six when Sam Woods joined him. The pair added 60 in only 40 minutes and this swung the game in Somerset's favour. Lionel was seventh out, caught in the slips, after batting two and three quarter hours for his 80, and Somerset went on to a narrow, two wicket victory.

After a draw with Yorkshire, Lionel made a rare guest appearance for the Somerset Stragglers making 124 against Chetnole Chappies. His lobs also captured eight wickets in the match, including his former teammate William Roe. This led nicely to the last Championship match at Taunton against Surrey. In an exciting match, yet again after rain had fallen heavily overnight, the pitch initially was drying out under a hot sun. As was the norm Surrey elected to bat and thanks to Ernie Hayes' unbeaten 86, Surrey managed 170 against some fine bowling by Cranfield and Braund.

With the wicket still difficult Lionel carried his bat for 45 out of 126, with only Gill (29) lasting long, Lionel's innings included six fours, and did not contain one faulty stroke. By the close of the first day Surrey progressed to 32 for one. On an easier wicket on the second day, Surrey made 252 setting Somerset a challenging 297 to win with well over a day remaining.

After losing Lewis with the score at three, Lionel was joined by Braund. Both of them started well and within 50 minutes the 50 was signalled. Lionel then increased the tempo with some lovely drives and cuts. Braund went for 47, having added 96 in 70 minutes. Lionel reached his fifty in an hour and a half. He was eventually dismissed for 77, fifth out at 160, having batted for two hours and ten minutes, and not giving a chance. After his dismissal, with the game in the balance, George Gill (64) and some tail contributions ensured a two wicket victory for Somerset.

This brought Somerset's and Lionel's season to an end. Somerset had a fairly good season winning seven and losing seven as they finished a creditable joint seventh, with Kent the champions. The main success was down to Braund and Cranfield as they both easily passed 100 wickets for the county.

For Lionel it had been a difficult season; it took him until the last couple of matches to really find his form and he failed to score a century for the first time since 1897. He finished the season with 1,119 runs at 30.24, with only five half centuries to his name. Despite this he was offered a place on the 1902-03 tour to Australia but turned it down for family and business reasons. In November he was elected President of Taunton Athletic Club. At Somerset County Cricket Club's annual general meeting, the club announced a profit thanks largely due to the visiting Australians.

By spring of 1903 Lionel was elected as Vice-President of Taunton Vale Foxhounds. He was like his father becoming an important member of many sporting bodies. These, with his work and family commitments, would start to limit his time for playing for the county. The year 1903 would be the first real indication that work came before cricket.

He warmed up for the first county game with two minor matches in poor weather; his only innings for Somerset Stragglers ended with him bowled for six. The first county game of the season brought the visit of Yorkshire; yet again Somerset beat the northern county, this time by six wickets with Lionel contributing 43 and 11, Braund with 47 and 14 plus ten wickets having a major say.

Against Middlesex Lionel made 56 in the first innings adding 96 with Braund, but an indifferent second innings batting effort resulted in a 112-run defeat. Lionel followed this with a duck against Lancashire in a drawn game badly affected by the weather.

On June 20, an interview with him appeared in the *Dundee Courier*. In the article (some comments by Lionel are strange), he starts by comparing hunting to cricket. He also complains that drawn cricket matches are a disease and advocated that all teams should play to win and not promote boring draws. He also advocated a change to the leg before wicket law, to stop players just padding balls not straight (it took until the 1930s for this to happen); he also thought bats were too wide and should be narrowed.

He would return to the Somerset side at the end of June to play the visiting Philadelphians. Somerset won by ten wickets, with Lionel making a quick 46 in the second innings. The team then beat Gloucestershire at Bath, but Lionel then missed the whole of July to business and family commitments.

He returned against Middlesex at Taunton, as Somerset narrowly lost by two wickets, Lionel making 21 in each innings. He showed better form in the next game against Sussex scoring 54 and 46 but the game was left drawn as Somerset batted all the last day making 419 for eight. After Lionel made two against Kent in another drawn game, Worcestershire came to Taunton. Worcestershire were bowled for 186. On a pitch giving help to bowlers Lionel was to go on the offensive and although giving a few chances made 97 out of 154. Despite trailing by 32 runs on first innings, Cranfield and Braund spun Worcestershire out for 72 and Somerset ran out winners by four wickets.

The penultimate game of the season for Somerset soon followed at Taunton against Surrey. After winning the toss the first day barely saw an hour's play as Somerset closed on 67 for one with Lionel on 26. With Johnson he took their partnership to 120 on the second morning before Lionel fell for 67. Somerset gained a lead of 73 on the first innings. Somerset started the second innings on the final day with a result unlikely. Nevertheless Lionel in fine style hit 114 with 14 fours. Somerset declared as the game petered out to a draw.

Somerset finished on a high by beating Hampshire with Lionel failing in each innings. Braund with a century and eight wickets in the match had a key say in the 109-run win. Somerset again won as many as they lost, six, as they finished tenth, a drop of three places. Braund and Cranfield again bowling well were instrumental in many of the victories.

For Lionel it was a shortened season, as a result he made only 637 runs at 35.38, to finish 21st in the national averages.

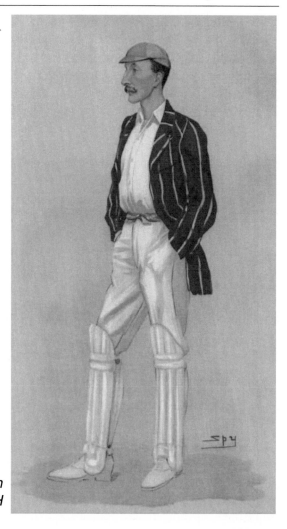

*A Spy cartoon
of LCH*

In September it was reported in the *Bath Courier* that he had entered a croquet competition in Bath. He lost 19-13 in the first round; later in the month he fared better, reaching the third round. This could have been the prequel to him starting to play golf, as by 1906 he was certainly playing golf and had given up croquet.

He attended the Somerset AGM where the club announced a big loss; the guarantors agreed to meet the shortfall. The local press stated that without these members the club would have folded; worrying times, that would continue for years.

The year 1904 started with Lionel taking part in some point-to-point competitions; he also became Honorary Secretary to Taunton Vale Foxhounds. In early April Len Braund was asked for his comments on Somerset's prospects; he was very pessimistic. To make it worse Cranfield was ill in hospital. Cranfield often suffered from ill health, and his form fell away until 1908 and he would die from pneumonia in 1909. It was also reported that Lionel would not be available until August due to work commitments; as it turned out he played all season.

He only played one warm-up game before the season, turning out for Taunton against Bridgwater. Although he was dismissed by Braund for 17, he got revenge by bowling Braund and trapping his captain Sam Woods lbw.

His first appearance of the season was against Gloucestershire at Bristol. After an even first innings, Lionel opened the second innings with Braund. In a stay of four and half hours he was to score 166 out of 310. He was missed three times (on 42, 45 and 109). The majority of his runs were from clean hard drives, his main hits being 13 fours and ten threes. The innings closed for 310, setting Gloucestershire 298 to win. After a keen struggle Gloucestershire got home by three wickets. The match though would be remembered for one over bowled by Len Braund; Gilbert Jessop hit him for 28 runs (446446), then a world record.

Lionel had a quiet time over the next three games, until the visit of Lancashire to Bath in early June. Going in for the second innings Somerset were facing an innings defeat as Lancashire led by 250 runs. For Somerset Cranfield had recovered enough to have made his return after the defeat to Gloucestershire. Lionel and Braund opening made a great effort to turn the match around. Lionel started poorly and struggled against Walter Brearley's short balls; Braund at the other end started in fine style as he hit 35 of the first 50 after an hour. At 23 Lionel gave a chance at long-off as Les Poidevin just failed to hold the ball; shortly afterwards Lionel should have been run out. Despite this his innings gained momentum and Lionel reached his half century after 70 minutes. Immediately he was again dropped, this time by Harold Garnett, who running back dropped the ball as he tried to hold the catch over his head. The pair though continued their partnership until it reached 161, when Braund (84) was caught; the partnership had lasted only an hour and three-quarters. At the close Somerset were 178 for one with Lionel on 88.

The following morning he completed his century having been at the crease for two and a quarter hours. He was to fall shortly afterwards to Brearley for 113. Sadly the innings fell away and Somerset could only make 277; Lancashire soon hit off the runs without loss.

Before his next Somerset game, he turned out firstly for Somerset Stragglers and made an unbeaten 153 against Devon Dumplings; he then took five wickets for Leighton against Bath, and for Sam Woods' eleven against Bath and District he scored 86. During this innings he hit Braund three times for six and a four in one over. Braund did have the edge though, as he made 176 as his team won.

Lionel would carry this form into the next game against Worcestershire at New Road, in what is possibly the finest innings he ever played. Winning the toss Worcestershire were restricted to 174, thanks largely to Braund who finished with eight for 81. With nearly three hours until stumps. Lionel opened with Braund. Lionel immediately started hitting the bowling, mainly in front of the wicket with some superb drives. The pair added 119 at over a run a minute before Braund fell for 36. Lewis then came in and Lionel carried on, reaching his hundred at almost a run a minute. Lewis (33) left at 223, the second wicket having added 104. At this point wickets started to fall regularly. Lionel held firm and by the close was unbeaten on 197, with Somerset closing on 314 for seven. The second morning began in sunny weather; Lionel started with a four to bring up his double hundred made in three hours. He was caught shortly afterwards for 203. He hit 30 fours and gave no chance, in a brilliant display of forcing, controlled cricket. Worcestershire, facing arrears of 178, fell apart in their second attempt as Cranfield and Braund shared the wickets. They slumped to 64 all out, Somerset gaining an easy victory by an innings and 114.

Somerset then started their northern tour, firstly to Hull to play Yorkshire. After Woods elected to bat Lionel opened with Braund and again showed brilliant form, as he hit his 50 out of

67 in three quarters of an hour. The score rose to 120 in an hour and a quarter, before he was caught behind for 70 off Haigh. The press noted 'his innings was full of cuts and some splendid drives which he always kept on the ground'. Somerset closed on 302. Yorkshire only headed this by 26 on their first innings. Going in a second time Lionel was first out for 25; Somerset struggled to 176 and lost easily by seven wickets.

The county fared worse as they moved onto Manchester. Somerset could only post 166 in their first innings and Lancashire ran up 580, with four players making a century. Trailing by 414, Lionel and Braund opened and attacked from the first ball. The partnership soon went to 75, in only 40 minutes, when Braund was dismissed for 25. Lionel soon reached his 40 in as many minutes. He continued in fine fashion until he was beaten by a 'bailer' from Alexander Kermode; he had made 81 in 70 minutes. Somerset went on to lose by an innings.

Lionel then played a couple of non-first class matches for the MCC; he made 105 in the win over Wiltshire and 27 and 21 in the draw against Glamorgan. He also took three wickets in the match with his lobs. Somerset were then beaten by an innings by the touring South Africans, Lionel, (five and one) having a poor match, a far cry from the victory against them in 1901.

Somerset restored pride in the next game with an easy 222-run win over Hampshire in a high-scoring match, with well over 1,100 runs scored. Lionel contributed a useful 57 in the first innings. Lewis (101 and 97) narrowly missed being the first player to score a century in each innings for Somerset.

Over the next five games Lionel failed to pass 50, and the team managed only one win, over Surrey at the Oval by an innings. His next innings of any note was against Kent at Taunton. After an innings each Kent had a slender lead of 16; however at their second attempt they ran up 401, setting Somerset an unlikely 418 to win, with about five hours left. Somerset's only hope was to play for a draw. For some reason Woods changed the batting order, which proved a bad move, as within half an hour they had been reduced to 20 for four. Braund batting at six and Lionel at five were now together. Both batted freely and within 95 minutes had added 116 for the fifth wicket. Lionel fell for 79, having played faultlessly and hitting ten fours, many superb drives. Somerset lost at the start of the final hour.

Somerset then completed the double over Surrey by seven wickets at Taunton. Lionel made a useful 49 in the second innings. He added 59 in the innings defeat to Yorkshire. The final match of the season against Hampshire was a tame draw, with Lionel finishing the season making only nine.

Lionel though had had a good season, scoring 1,277 runs at 37.55, the seventh and last time he would score a thousand runs in a season. He achieved this feat six times for Somerset. From a team perspective it had been a fairly poor season; although five matches were won, eleven were lost. Part of the reason was the falling off of Braund and Cranfield as bowlers; the batting was inconsistent and regularly collapsed; and poor team displays were becoming common. The county eventually finished twelfth, a drop of two places on 1903.

As the season finished Lionel played a croquet doubles tournament in Bath, eventually losing in the third round. In November Somerset held its AGM. With Lionel sitting in the chair the club announced a loss again. Later in the month was possibly the first sign of him wanting to move as he travelled to Devon to attend a county ball.

Chapter seven
Captain of Somerset, and the Earl of Devon

In January 1905, Lionel announced that he had been appointed as land agent to KR Miller-Mundy's estates in Shipley, Derbyshire, and as a result it was unlikely that he could play regularly or possibly ever play for Somerset again. He resigned from his numerous committees in the county. He announced 'it was business first pleasure second'. For the county this was extremely bad news, as effectively the county had lost three notable amateur batsmen for 1905: JL Daniell was tea planting in India and FA Phillips was in Africa in the Army. There were no players on the horizon that the county thought could be useful. The notice of his intentions to virtually give up the game were reported in *Cricket; A Weekly Record of the Game* in May.

Also that month, it was reported that his brother Richard and father Henry had registered a patent for a turbine; as there is no follow-up to this or mention of it again, I can only assume the invention did not take off, and make them the money they had hoped. Then on June 7, the *Lancashire Evening Post* reported Lionel's surprise announcement that he was to return to the south and move to Devon as he had just accepted the post as land agent to the Earl of Devon at Powderham Castle in Exeter; he would take up his post in October. It was also mentioned that it was unlikely he would be able to play much again.

The acceptance of the role would mean that Lionel would stay with the Earl of Devon for the rest of his working life. Lionel was employed by the fourteenth Earl of Devon, Charles Pepys Courtenay (1870-1927). The earl and Lionel will have known each other, as the earl was a keen Somerset supporter and one of the guarantors who helped make good the annual losses the club generally made.

The earl's residence was Powderham Castle, a fortified manor house in the parish of Exminster, about six miles to the south of the county town, Exeter. To the north-east of the castle the main gates lead to the village of Kenton. An earl is still in residence, and the eighteenth Earl has only passed away in 2015. Lionel and his family would live in a big house that he would call 'Kenton

Lodge' in the village. The size of Lionel's house can be gleaned from the 1911 census as he had six servants within the household.

His work for Lord Devon was varied. He helped settle disputes, renovate property, buy and sell land or houses and organise any building work. Many adverts regarding his work for the earl appeared in local papers over the years. In addition, he would join a number of committees as time passed, and he would attend local council, golf club and Conservative Party meetings and was an active member of the Fisheries Commission. It was clear that on moving there in autumn 1905, he quickly became part of the local community and a leading well-respected figure within Devon.

Despite a lot of changes in his life in 1905, Lionel did have time for a little cricket. Whilst in Derbyshire he played a little for Welbeck and turned out once for the Old Reptonians against his old school. Although he did little with the bat against Repton he took the wicket of John Crawford, the brilliant schoolboy cricketer who would later play for Surrey and England.

Lionel's move to Devon also meant he would be able to play a couple of times for Somerset. The press knew in advance of his return and it was announced, a month beforehand, of his intention to play against the visiting Australians. On July 13 the Australians ran up 609 for four with Warwick Armstrong making an unbeaten 303. Somerset were largely in debt to Len Braund and Henry Martyn as they both made centuries, and although following on, Somerset were able to save the game easily. Lionel made four, and two not out. The game was also noted for the appearance of Tom Richardson the former Surrey fast man, released by Surrey the year before. He had taken a pub in Bath and was persuaded by Sam Woods to turn out. It had been hoped he could contribute with the ball. However he was grossly overweight, bowled barely medium pace and went wicketless, a sad end to a fine career.

Although Lionel did not play for another month, he returned to Taunton against Kent in mid-August. After Woods elected to bat on a good wicket, Lionel went in with the team struggling at 34 for three. He started cautiously and struggled against the opening bowlers Jack Mason and Colin Blythe at first. He settled in and started to play in his old form, one hit from Bill Fairservice going over the sightscreen. However as he gained momentum the side lost wickets. When the last man John Harcombe came to the wicket Lionel was on 85. Trying to force the game, Lionel was stumped for 91. His innings had lasted two hours and 25 minutes. After Somerset closed on 231, Kent ran up 539 and went on to win by an innings. Lionel made 20 second time round. He played one more game against Warwickshire, but made only nine in a drawn game.

On the pitch Somerset had a very poor season. With Northamptonshire admitted to the County Championship there were now 16 clubs. Somerset finished fifteenth with only one win and ten losses. In addition, the club made a loss of £454 (£45,000 in 2016 money); had it not been for the Australian match it would have been over £1,400 (£140,000 in 2016). As a result, the guarantors agreed to contribute £3 each; this would raise £420 and the balance would be made up of fund-raising. Sam Woods clearly had had enough and wanted to resign, but at the AGM was persuaded to carry on for another year. With no new talent on the horizon and many key players missing or losing form, the outlook did not look good.

The *Wells Journal* in April 1906 was very pessimistic before Somerset's campaign; they did however state Lionel would be back as a regular. Sadly he only was to play once. It was clear that Lionel was concentrating on settling in to his new job. His first recorded cricket that year was on July 5 as he made a duck playing for Major DF Bowles' eleven against the Devon Regiment. A fortnight later he was in a car crash when his vehicle collided with a motorcycle; happily no one was hurt. Local press reports do not give any indication how it happened.

He played two other minor matches without any notable score, before he turned out for his only game that season for Somerset. The opponents were Yorkshire at Bath. The match was won by Yorkshire by 389 runs. George Hirst, who was to take 200 wickets and score 2,000 runs in the season (the only player ever to do this), had a fine match, with a century in each innings and taking eleven wickets. Lionel was actually captain as Woods was absent, having picked up a strain. Lionel top scored for Somerset in each innings making 31 and 42. Somerset did have a better season winning four games and climbing to eleventh. Lionel also is recorded as playing golf at The Warren near his home in Kenton; but he would not compete yet for another two years. He did enter the Teignmouth Croquet Championships but lost in the third round. On December 1, he attended the Somerset AGM. The club news was bleak. Losses for the year had increased to £900 (£87,000 in 2016 money). Again guarantors picked up most of the losses and the balance would be covered by a fund-raising event to be held in the spring. The club passed a resolution to save costs; this would mean fewer professional players, and would compound the club's weakness on the field.

Lionel also raised the issue of the county not producing their own players and that the club needed to do something to help find and develop young players. As a result, the meeting agreed to set up a team called Somerset Juniors and the club would invite promising young players in the county to play in matches. All committee men were encouraged to go back to their districts and identify possible future players. As a result, up to the outbreak of the Second World War the Somerset Juniors would play a number of matches each season. Early players to be identified were William Greswell and Jack White. But it helped spot and develop many others; these included Reggie Ingle, Bunty Longrigg and Harold Gimblett.

Sam Woods again resigned as captain. He was struggling physically but his contribution to the team was also negligible; he did not bowl any more and his batting average was less than 20; injuries were causing him to miss more and more games, he was heavier in weight and approaching 40. Lord Devon, a vice-president of the club, agreed to release Lionel for one year to stand in as captain for 1907 only. It was hoped that the club could get on a better financial footing, find a captain, and hopefully have some success on the field. It was also agreed to give Len Braund a benefit (which took place in 1908). The meeting closed with the knowledge that if the scale of losses continued for another season then the county would have to fold, the omens for Lionel's captaincy for 1907 and the club did not look good.

Before the season even started, Somerset lost a key player who was blossoming into a fine bat; Henry Martyn retired due to business commitments. In 1906 he had become the first Somerset wicket-keeper to score 1,000 runs in a season. Somerset could not afford the loss of a fine batsman and a high quality wicket-keeper. In the *Taunton Courier* on April 3, it was stated that the prospects of a good season for Somerset were very bleak; sadly this would unfold over the season.

Apart from captaining school, and two seasons when at Oxford, Lionel had not captained any side. In addition he had only played a few first class games since 1904 and very little minor cricket. It would be a test of not only his captaincy, but also whether he had retained enough of his skill to be able to lead from the front. In hindsight it was asking a lot of him. To make the matter harder, he played no minor cricket and relied on net practice only; this was not to work. The reason was probably that he still had to keep up to his duties for the earl when not playing for Somerset.

The first game of the season was at Taunton against Yorkshire, starting on May 9. Not surprisingly Somerset went down by nine wickets. Len Braund though carried his bat for 42 out of 113 in the second innings. In his first game as captain Lionel made 17 and one. The team then travelled to Tonbridge to play Kent. Winning the toss Lionel opened with Braund in dull and rather chilly weather. The side made a terrible start losing Braund and Lewis to successive balls from Arthur Fielder, who should have had a hat-trick but Bill Montgomery was dropped by the keeper Fred Huish. Despite this Lionel seemed to find his old form as he drove and cut well. He reached his 50 in seventy minutes, with the score 71 for four. He held the side together and at lunch was still in with the score 161 for eight. He completed his hundred in two hours and 15 minutes, and was last out for 116, having hit 16 fours, out of only 192. Little did he know it but this was the last of his 27 first-class centuries, and he would not pass 50 again for the next 25 innings. Somerset then bowled Kent out for 131 to gain a lead of 61, but going in a second time the team was routed by Fielder and Blythe for 72. Kent easily knocked the runs off for the loss of only two wickets.

The next game at Lord's went down in history. Albert Trott the faithful Australian professional had chosen the game for his benefit. After an innings apiece Somerset only trailed by 50 runs and then bowled Middlesex for 213, setting Somerset a testing, but possible 264 runs for victory and they had a full day to get them. Opening, Lionel and Braund scored freely until the introduction of Trott with the score at 53. Lionel fell to Tarrant for a forceful 35. The score progressed to 77 for three when the fireworks from Trott began. He trapped Lewis lbw second ball, then spread-eagled Massey Poyntz' stumps, completing his hat-trick by bowling Woods. Amidst great excitement he made it four in four as he bowled Ernie Robson. Trott was not finished as at 97 for seven he completed the second hat-trick of the innings. Somerset lost by 166 runs; Len Braund again carried his bat for 28 and the innings was all over in 95 minutes. Trott finished with seven for 20.

Happily, Somerset then won their first game against Sussex at Taunton by six wickets, Lionel contributing, thanks to some fine drives and cuts, with 49 he dominated an opening stand of 69 with Braund. This improved form seemed to be maintained in the next game at Bath. Again after one innings each, Somerset only trailed by six runs. In the second innings Somerset were well placed at 146 for two, but the dismissal of Braund resulted in the team only adding another 40 runs. Lancashire struggled to put together partnerships thanks from some good team bowling; at 159 for eight, with still another 23 needed, Somerset had a chance, but Thomas Higson and Harry Dean held their nerve and saw Lancashire home.

The recent upturn in form was not continued. Somerset were well beaten by six wickets by Worcestershire, who were having a fine season and would finish joint second to unbeaten Nottinghamshire. Somerset's next game was the return at Worcestershire. In much better batting form the side gained a respectable draw. The game was notable for the first-class debut of Bertie Bisgood who made 82 and 116 not out. Sadly he could not continue this as in 67 games for the county he had a batting average of less than 19.

Somerset then started their northern tour at Headingley with an innings defeat. In the second innings Lionel (47) and Braund (34) opened with a good stand of 83; little more than an hour later the side were all out for 122. This defeat prompted the *Bath Chronicle* to add that after the openers were gone Somerset's batting was weak; it would not get any better as time would show. Another innings defeat followed at Manchester against Lancashire. Lionel ran himself out for nought in the first innings and on their way back the team drew with Warwickshire as the match was badly spoilt by rain. Lionel's bad run continued as he made only six in his only innings.

The weather again spoilt the next game at Bristol. Despite both Lionel and Gilbert Jessop using declarations to try and force a result, the game ended with Somerset with two wickets left, requiring 13 to win. Happily back on home turf at Bath, the team registered their second win of the season as they romped home by seven wickets against Warwickshire. Braund's match analysis of 14 for 141 was the main factor as he bowled in his form of a few years previously.

Somerset then travelled to Hastings and lost by nine wickets, best remembered for the reappearance of the slow left-arm bowler, Ted Tyler, as he took nine for 83; however it was only to be a flash in the pan. Lionel's 43 in the second innings was his best innings for some time. Returning to Taunton a close game looked on the cards as after one innings each, Somerset held a slender lead of 18. Gloucestershire were then skittled by Lewis and Mordaunt for only 37. Somerset though lost four wickets getting the 20 needed.

A crushing innings defeat to Middlesex followed. Braund again carried his bat (67 out of 226). Lionel after a poor run had dropped down to four. The only note of cheer was Peter Johnson and Frank Phillips, back in the team to bolster the batting until the end of the season. After a drought of over two months Lionel made 78 against Hampshire in the first innings. An unbeaten 71 form Robson, who then took seven for 60, helped set up a lead of 59. However Somerset's 95 all out resulted in an eight wicket loss after another dismal batting display.

Lionel's return to form continued as he made 62 against Kent, but the side were soundly thrashed by an innings. The last Championship games resulted in Hampshire performing the double, and the last fixture against the tourists South Africa ended a miserable season as the side lost by 358 runs. Lionel signed off with seven and nought, his form and patience with the team being at a low ebb. This was confirmed by his comments at the Somerset's annual meeting at the end of the season in December.

Somerset in 1907, a difficult and unhappy year for Lionel. Back: CG Deane, HE Murray-Anderdon, BL Bisgood, AE Lewis, PR Johnson, HF Montgomery, E Robson, AE Bailey. Front: EJ Tyler, SMJ Woods, LCH Palairet, AE Newton, LC Braund

Somerset finished the season fourteenth. With the bat Lionel had a very poor season. Despite only scoring 768 runs at 21.33, he still finished fourth in the county averages, a reflection of how poor a batting team they were. Lack of top level match practice, and I think the pressures of the role affected his batting. There are also reports that he was quite aloof and not encouraging to players; he certainly was not helped by so many players representing the county, many with poor records; and the more experienced players were generally past their best.

As early as September 3 in the *Plymouth Gazette*, it was reported that Lionel would be standing down as captain; it had been clear he was only temporary for a year anyway. The newspaper added that he was to play possibly for Exeter and Devon next season. It transpired neither was correct; perhaps it was Lionel reporting this, as he was clearly frustrated about the season he had just endured.

In early December, at Somerset's AGM, it was confirmed that Lionel would not continue as captain. As John Daniell had returned from India, he was appointed for 1908. Happier news was reported that due to the cost-cutting the club was in surplus; however the fixture list would be reduced from 18 to 16 matches after 1909. Somerset on the field were in dreadful trouble and there was even talk of dropping into the minor counties: the club had no money, continuing losses, only three professionals, no new talent and dwindling support. Somehow though the club would continue mainly through the efforts of the committee and loyal members who shared the losses each season up to the Great War. It's little surprise that Lionel, and then Daniell and Poyntz, had poor records as captain. The plain truth was that the team was not good enough to compete at Championship level. There was too much for too few of the capable players to do, day in and day out.

The *Taunton Gazette* published Lionel's thoughts on the season. He stated:

'This season is the most disappointing I have ever had to face in my life. Throughout the season this team has had no fighting spirit, there is a distinct lack of ability and the team is ageing with no talent coming through to compete at a first class level.'

Quite damning but true. The *Taunton Courier* went on to add that 'in recent seasons the County has paid for professionals from other counties, and sadly none of these candidates show any real ability to contribute on a daily basis, the last recruit who was successful was Braund and that was some years ago.' Lionel may well have been relieved to be getting out; for the county bleaker years lay ahead. Lionel would now pretty much throw his lot in with Devon, mainly playing golf.

Chapter eight
Devon, golf and the War

Free from captaincy, it was hoped that Lionel could still assist Somerset when available; this seemed to hold during 1908. He turned out against Warwickshire at the end of May, when Somerset won easily, although he contributed little with the bat. A few weeks later he made useful 46 against Gloucestershire in a game that was eventually drawn.

Lionel also played in the following game against Hampshire at Bath. In the follow-on, he batted at four and in fine style reached his 50 in 70 minutes, showing much of his old flair and scoring in fine style. At the end of the day he had reached 51, although at 117 for five, Somerset were still looking at probable defeat. The following morning he started nervously and was dropped three times before falling to a magnificent catch on the boundary for 77. This would be his last fifty in a first-class match.

He made three more appearances that summer, but his only other innings of note was 40 against Middlesex in a draw at Taunton, a game memorable for the batting of Peter Johnson who made 164 and 131, to become the first Somerset batsman to score a century in each innings. Lionel did play in some minor matches. On July 3, he appeared for Free Forresters against Devon Regiment in a two day game which formed part of the annual Devon cricket week, which was generally played at Exeter. For the next 15 years this would form the main part of his cricket season. He scored 48 and 118 as his team won. In the second innings, he put on over 150 for the first wicket with his old Somerset friend Sammy Woods.

In the second game of the week, he raised his own LCH Palairet eleven to play Devon at Exeter in a three day game. In the first innings he hit a brilliant 143, which included a six and 16 fours. Also in his team was Ernest Robson, Prince Narayan and Leslie Gay, all Somerset colleagues. His side went on to win. Devon may have wished he would play for them.

So brought the close of another cricket season. Under John Daniell's captaincy, Somerset slipped to the bottom of the Championship for the first time. The team only won one of its

20 matches. *Wisden* described Somerset's season in two words: 'a disaster'. Lionel by the year end was building links with Devon County Cricket Club, attending meetings which discussed the possibility of inviting the Australians to play a game in the county. However due to the cost of the game, and the likelihood the county would lose money, it was decided not to follow up. The actual vote ended 9-9 with the chairman casting the deciding vote. Lionel was very much in favour of the visit.

By November, there is the first record of Lionel playing in golf tournaments. From then until his death he appeared in various tournaments; friendly club matches; and ultimately for his new county, Devon. He played most of his golf for The Warren Club, which still exists in the Devon seaside town of Dawlish. In December, it was on this course that he tied for first with CF Titjen in the club's Monthly Medal Cup, out of 21 entries. His handicap at this point was nine.

By 1909, there are records of tournaments he entered at least every month. In July he again tied for first with CF Titjen; by now his handicap had dropped to six. By the end of the year he was also entering open tournaments, playing doubles, and mixed doubles with his wife. He also started playing for Warren against other golf clubs in friendly matches; this meant a game of singles and foursomes. In his first recorded game Warren beat Churchston 10-2 with Lionel winning both games.

As a result of playing golf nearly each weekend he played little cricket. There are no records of him playing any minor matches, though he did have two more matches for Somerset. Sadly he failed to make double figures in any game. In his final match against Kent he made one, and three run out, a sad way to end such a distinguished career. By now though Lionel was clearly concentrating on his golf; he would only play a little country house cricket.

By the end of 1910, his handicap was down to one, and he won two more tournaments at Warren. It was this year that the Palairet Cup was played for at Warren each year. The winner of this cup was deemed the Devon amateur champion; the cup is still played for annually. Lionel would occasionally play in the competition. His cricket was limited to only four matches, and his only innings

LCH in reflective mood

of note was in making 74 for Mr Gibbs' eleven against Sidmouth.

Lionel though was still following Somerset. In 1911 the club granted HE Murray-Anderdon a testimonial as he was standing down as honorary secretary of the club, which was still struggling financially. A committee was set up including Lionel and old players Herbie Hewett, Sam Woods and John Daniell to raise funds as thanks to Murray-Anderdon, for all his years of service to Somerset. This year saw a big drop in the golf and cricket Lionel played; his handicap increased to four and there is only a record of one appearance on the cricket field.

He also became the first chairman of the Devon County Golf Union. The meeting was held at the Queen's Hotel, Exeter on October 26. The union was made up initially of 19 clubs with Lionel representing Warren. It's from this meeting that he would be immortalised with the creation of the Palairet Cup.

In February 1912, he was elected to Devon County Council, increasing his position within the community and county. His golfing career was back on track as by February he became a scratch golfer and was one of the best amateurs in the county. He won two more competitions and played over 20 various tournaments during the year. The following year he was the secretary of Warren Club, attending all Devon golfing meetings for them. He again had a successful year winning three individual tournaments and with WRC Laverton, one of his brother-in-laws, his first doubles title.

In September, he made his golf county debut for Devon at Burnham-on-Sea against Somerset. Devon lost 5-3 as he lost his singles match to RW May by one hole. He was given the honour of county captain. Lionel was also active on the cricket field playing a number of single and two day games. Playing for Seaton against Upper Tooting he scored 131 and took six wickets in a two day match; he also scored two other fifties and regularly bowled his lobs. Late in the year he helped his team Warren to win the inter-club Foursomes Cup; he would repeat this feat again in 1914 and 1920, on each occasion with his old partner KF Fradgley.

By 1914, he was continuing to play in a number of tournaments throughout the year. In July he again played against Somerset in a county match, now captain of Devon, and after a break for the war, he would resume the captaincy from 1920 until 1926. This time Devon won by eight and a half to three and a half. Lionel won his singles five and four against Captain Armstrong but lost his foursome match. He also played for Devon Amateurs versus Devon Professionals. The match ended in a draw 11-11; he halved his singles match but with Kenneth Fradgley easily won the foursomes. With Fradgley, he became Devon foursome's champions as they won the Gold Medal at Warren.

The outbreak of war put a halt to his sporting activities. In October he attended the Somerset county cricket AGM. Since Lionel had retired the club had been bottom of the Championship three times. Massey Poyntz had taken over the captaincy from Daniell in 1913. Gerald Fowler the long-suffering treasurer reported a loss of £600 (2016 equivalent, £58,000). With Henry (Lionel's father) in the chair it was then discussed that the club's future was in serious doubt.

From the meeting there was a strong indication that the debenture holders might close the club. Lionel asked how the club could avoid this, as if it occurred, the club would close forever. Fowler stated that the club needed £100 to carry on until Christmas. Three committees were set up, based in Weston super Mare, Taunton and Bath. Each committee of four members was solely to raise funds to try and keep the club going until the war was over.

In January 1915 the club met again, still £600 in debt, but due to guarantors it had managed to keep going. It was also acknowledged that the club would not play any matches during 1915, as there was obviously little chance of an end soon to the war. The club then agreed to try and collect subscriptions from existing members, and due to the fact that there would be a much reduced expenditure bill, it was hoped that this would reduce the overdrawn £600 and ensure the club could keep going. The club guarantors stated they would guarantee any debt if debentures holders or the bank did foreclose on the club. The club stated that it did not want the guarantors to yet again subsidise the club's losses. Surprisingly, the club nominated AE Newton, the old wicket-keeper who was now 52, to be the captain for 1915.

Lionel was too old to enlist, aged 45 in 1915, though you could enlist up to 50 if you had a special skill. Lionel was given command at Remount Depot at Powderham; he would help supply the Army and raise funds within the area.

A number of former players over-age did apply, and were accepted by the Army. His younger brother Richard by March was captain of a battalion. In July the *Western Gazette* listed a number of county players serving in the Army: these included Walter Hedley, Herbert Hewett, Vernon Hill, and the Rippon twins. The newspaper also reported the death of former bowler Frank Joy, a mistake however as he survived the war and lived until 1966.

As a result of the war it appears though Lionel kept in practice there were no golf tournaments. His only cricket match each year was for MCC against Clifton College at Bristol. Generally the MCC took a strong side and many old players would turn out; these included Lord Hawke, JH Board, GJ Thompson, JT Hearne and FH Huish. Lionel's only innings of note was in 1915 when he made 52; he did however take some wickets with his lobs.

In December 1915, Lionel attended the Somerset County Cricket Club AGM. It was announced losses had fallen from £600 to £342, so the club could continue. An appeal would be made to members to continue to pay subscriptions while the war went on. This would continue and as a result the club could take part in the 1919 Championship; had the members not paid, Somerset would have folded.

By 1917, Lionel was spending a lot of time on food committees and helping organise events to raise funds for the war. In April 1918 he joined the committee of the MCC. In December he went with Murray-Anderdon to represent Somerset and help arrange the fixtures for the 1919 season, as the war had finally ended in November. At the meeting it was agreed all county games would be played over two days with an early start and late finish; this was not popular and only lasted for that season.

Chapter nine
Committees and playing for Devon

With the end of the war Lionel could concentrate a little more on playing golf and playing some cricket. For the MCC against Clifton College he made 103; playing in his old form he hit a six and 15 fours. By September he was back playing in golf tournaments and his handicap would be back to scratch within a year.

In August 1919 the *Bath Chronicle* did a feature about his batting style, saying 'His batting was a thing of joy, every shot executed with a minimum of exertion and maximum power'. The newspaper concluded that he retired too early and there were no batsman of the day with his grace and style. The paper added that 'he could play a half-cocked shot to a shooter (Trumper's dog shot), this helped him bat on a sticky wicket although he was a front foot player'.

By 1920 he was back on various work and golf committees and still working for the Earl of Devon. In April he won a golf doubles tournament with WRC Laverton, and on the cricket field he hit 64 and 62 for the MCC against Devon Club and Ground at Exeter in late August. Life for everyone was now getting back to normal.

The following year, in June he travelled with his wife aboard the SS Mauretania from Southampton to New York for a holiday in America, and in December his daughter married. Although he did not win a golf tournament in 1921, he began to enter more doubles and individual events within the county. He also played his usual few games for the MCC, and Free Foresters, plus the odd scratch side at cricket. His best effort during 1921 was 48 and 71 for MCC against United Services at Devonport in late August.

The following year 1922 saw Lionel elected President of the Devon Golf Alliance. As a golfer he had his busiest year so far. He twice played for the county in May. Devon lost 6-3 to Dorset at Budleigh Salterton; Lionel lost his singles but managed a half at foursomes. In August, Devon beat Somerset 7-4, as Lionel won both his singles and foursomes this time. Although he again failed to win a competition he finished second in a couple of tournaments and lost in a couple of finals.

He also hit 171 for Free Foresters against Devon Regiment; the local press described it 'as a brilliant innings'. This would be the last known century made by him. His son Henry was also reported in a number of tennis competitions and played a few games of cricket for Devon Dumplings, although he seems not to have been much of a cricketer. He made only six runs in four innings, and also played a game with Lionel for the Free Foresters, bagging a pair. In December Lionel's stepmother Charlotte passed away. It was also reported that Lionel's father was giving up all his committees due to failing health; he apparently had a heart condition that was rapidly affecting his health. On March 20 the following year his father died, and was reported in most southern 'papers.

Although playing less competitive golf during the year Lionel still turned out for his county. In May, Devon beat Cornwall at St Endoc 9-6. He lost both of his matches quite easily. At Sidmouth later in the month, Devon romped to a 10-2 win over Somerset. This time, in better form Lionel won both of his games. In his third appearance in the year, in October at Burnham, Devon won a good match eight and a half to six and a half in the return against Somerset. He lost his singles badly to AJ Palmer (five and four), but won his foursomes with Kenneth Fradgley at the last hole. By now his handicap had gone up to three; he again failed to win a tournament. He did however enter some home-grown vegetables in a local competition, winning first prize for his potatoes.

His administrative skills in promoting and organising golf meant that by February 1924 he was elected vice-president of the newly formed South Western Golf Union; this looked after all counties in the region. His standing within the golfing world made him one of the best known people in the game. His wife was also busy as she was chaired the Local Unionist Association. Lionel had also joined the Liberal Party but by the end of the year was back as a loyal Conservative supporter.

On the cricket field he made his usual handful of appearances, making a useful 57 for Free Foresters against the Devon Regiment in July; and the following month 48 for the Devon Dumplings against Somerset Stragglers at Exeter.

He played a lot more golf during this year; in May he won the *Western Morning News* individual tournament, the tenth known win in his career. For Devon he lost both his singles and foursomes at Westward Ho! in late June as Dorset beat Devon 8-7. A few days later, again at Westward Ho!, Devon easily beat Somerset 13 and a half to ten and a half; this time Lionel won his singles but again lost out in his foursomes. The return against Somerset was played at Weston super Mare a month later. Devon won more emphatically 11 and a half to six and a half; this time Lionel reversed his results, losing his singles but easily winning the foursomes. Warren also won the club team championship, as Lionel, KF Fradgley and WH Shortt brought the trophy to the club for the first time.

In early 1925 he expanded his memberships on committees, to include being chairman of the Kenton and Powderham branch of the Conservative Party. However within a few months he then notified the party that he would have to stand down, as he intended to leave the parish as he planned to retire.

In February, the Devon Golf Union became part of the newly formed English Golf Union and Lionel unsurprisingly joined the new committee. This now meant he was a leading figure in the promoting and arranging of golf in England. Compared to his cricket career as an administrator his golf achievements were at least on a par; it is clear his golfing achievements and committee involvement meant a lot to him.

At the age of 55, though planning to retire he was still very active and pictures of him at this time still show him to be fairly slim and in good health. He appeared for Devon in four county golf games during the year. In March, Devon lost heavily 14-4 to Dorset with Lionel losing both games; later that month, even more crushingly the county went down 16-2 to Somerset; again Lionel went winless. However in late April, he did win a doubles competition partnering a 'Mr Jenkins'.

In October Lionel retired as land agent to the Earl of Devon. His retirement was reported in depth by the local press. Lord Devon thanked him for all his years of loyal service, presenting him with an inscribed silver tray. Lionel announced that he would now be residing in Cobham, Exeter. Shortly after he appeared at Torquay, as Devon beat Wiltshire nine and a half to five and a half, Lionel winning both his matches. Later in the week his local club Warren entertained Dorset. Devon reversed their humiliation earlier in the year, by winning nine and a half to five and a half, Lionel again winning both matches. His cricket was less successful; in four matches and five innings his highest score was only 11. His lack of regular practice, and his advancing age seemed now to be having a marked effect on his ability with the bat.

LCH right pictured in the Western Daily Express, *May 5, 1925, with KF Fradgley his regular golf foursomes partner for his club The Warren*

Chapter ten
The final years

At the age of 55, Lionel and his wife now could look forward to a long and happy retirement at their new home. Sadly like so many things in life it did not always go according to script. In his first year of retirement, Lionel concentrated on various committees and played as usual a lot of golf.

With his handicap now up to six, he again failed to win a competition. He did however play five times for his county. In March, Devon crushed Dorset 16 and a half to five and a half at Bournemouth, Lionel winning his foursomes but halving his singles match. A few days later he travelled to Bristol, as Gloucestershire won 9-6, Lionel losing both matches. Then in June at Lelant, Devon beat Cornwall 11-9 with Lionel winning two games to pick up two points. Later in the week at Yelverton, Somerset beat Devon 11-7, with only a half in the singles for Lionel. In his final game of the season for Devon at Budleigh Salterton, Devon beat Dorset 10-5. Lionel again halved his singles, but easily won his foursome match with a Mr Mitford as his doubles partner.

The 1926 season would be the last time that he played cricket. He played three matches: in late July he made 24 and 41 for the Free Foresters against Devon at Exeter, making some of his old trademark drives and cuts and showing good form for a man of his age. Again for the Free Foresters a month later he batted attractively for 29 and 31 against Sidmouth. His final competitive game was a benefit match for WT Cook's eleven against Sidmouth, a two day game in mid-September. After making a duck in the first innings, he again played some nice drives in making 31 in his final innings. The match included some notable players: WG Quaife (Warwickshire), JJ Bridges (Somerset), Jack Hobbs and Frank Woolley. Lionel's team lost by an innings, as Hobbs (102) and Woolley (134) made excellent centuries. It was a nice way for his cricket career to come to a close.

By 1927, the Palairets had settled into retirement well. Both children had now left home, and the Palairets now only employed a cook and two maids at their residence. Lionel played quite a bit of golf up to July. He again represented Devon, this time twice in July as they first beat Wiltshire 7-2, with Lionel winning his singles (foursomes were not played) and a few days later Devon beat 6-3 against Dorset, again Lionel winning his singles.

In July, he also attended a Varsity dinner reunion at The Savoy in London. This was to celebrate the centenary of the Oxford-Cambridge match. The event meant hundreds of former players attended, among them Lord Harris, Sam Woods and KJ Key. The press reported some attended the event who had played in the Varsity game over 50 years before. A number of speeches were made, and old friendships resumed from their college days. The press stated the dinner was a great success.

Lionel, having had a quiet 1927 regarding golf, resumed his career and in April with Mrs Mitford won a mixed doubles tournament at Budleigh Salterton. He was also to play his last county games for Devon. In June he won both his singles and foursomes as they easily beat Wiltshire 12-3. Later in the month he lost both his singles and foursomes as Gloucestershire narrowly won 8-7. He managed then to win his foursomes as they beat Cornwall 9-5.

It would appear though by the end of the year that his wife Caroline's health was failing. As a result he resigned from all his posts, except for his golfing committees. By November the couple had bought a house in Lansdown near Bath. His return to Somerset was noticed, and the Somerset county club made him the club president for 1929. His obsession with making a contribution to the community soon led him to be elected vice-president of Bath Cricket Club in March. The following month he was a noted guest at Gloucestershire County Cricket Club's annual dinner. Lionel also in March gave an interview to his local paper the *Exeter and Plymouth Gazette*. The newspaper commented that he had some interesting views on the current state of English cricket. In the article Lionel made the following comments:

'In the old days we used to score 200 runs before lunch comfortably. Today it takes a whole day play to attain that number. The public are getting sick and tired of slow scoring rates, and it cannot go on much longer. Crowds are down, only Australia and South Africa draw large crowds. Today's batting is nothing but siege mentality, players just dig in and try to wear bowling out, they seem to have forgotten the public pay to be entertained.

He blamed the war, 'as today's players did not come into contact with their fathers and grandfathers and what they had done for the game. He was optimistic that the old style would come back and players would play in the true spirit of the game and that was to entertain.' I wonder what he would have made of one-day cricket and T20.

Attending the Gloucestershire dinner, Lionel made another speech. He complained about the number of drawn games, saying there was too much cricket being played. The Gloucestershire Echo also reported that his speech 'was full of wit and anecdotes'. Despite the move, on September 9 his wife Caroline died; she was only 58. Lionel had only played two golf competitions that

LCH putting during a competition held at Sidmouth (Western Morning News) December 7, 1928

year and had been clearly looking after his wife, whose death was widely reported in the press.

Caroline's funeral took place at Westbury Parish Church on September 11. Only a few days later his sister Edith Scobell would also die, aged only 55. Still living in Bath and with a new decade starting, Lionel resumed an active season of playing golf; he would commute to Exeter to play in league games, and monthly tournaments throughout 1930. It was clear that his roots and many friends were still in Devon. Though he did not win anything, even at 60 he was still a good golfer and had six top ten finishes in singles competitions alone.

In January 1931, he had the honour of being elected president of the English Amateur Golf Union, the pinnacle of his golf administration and the highest honour that he could attain. It showed the recognition and admiration of others in the game. Within a month of receiving this honour, he was back in Devon and living in Exmouth, at a place he called 'Dodhill' a large house on Douglas Avenue; this would be his last move. Within the month he was back on the Devon Cricket Club committee attending meetings; he also remained president of the Devon Golf Union and English Golf Union, so although a widower he was still busy. Although he played fewer tournaments this year, he did win a doubles and mixed doubles tournament.

By 1932, he had limited most of his golf to representing his club Exmouth, playing against other golf teams within the county. He was very busy organising tournaments, and encouraging golf throughout the country. In November, he played in his last golf tournament. By January 1933 he was still active on golf committees, and in February he attended a school presenting various school prizes to the children. There was no indication that his health was in decline; he certainly showed no signs of slowing down.

On Thursday, March 24, he went to Portsmouth for a yachting trip with friends. On the Monday March 27, he returned by train and arrived at Exmouth station at 3pm. He then was driven home by a friend. After a short while, he went for a walk with his friend in his garden and collapsed without any warning. Two doctors, Dr De Glanville and Dr DLH Moore were summoned and arrived very promptly only to pronounce that he had already died. So at the relatively young age of 62 he was dead. His death appeared in most of the newspapers, often carrying comments about his fine work as a batsman but also as a golfer and keen administrator. On his funeral day, March 30, his aunt Laura Palairet passed away, she did however did live to a good age of 83.

His funeral took place at Littleham, Exmouth, the service conducted by the Rev TG Shelmerdine. Several hundred were at the funeral; his brother Richard was missing as he was co-manager of the MCC tour to Australia and New Zealand. The day before Lionel's death England had just drawn the First Test with New Zealand. The day after his funeral, the second Test commenced at Eden Park, Auckland, again the game was drawn, England batting far too long and slowly in each Test; this would not have pleased Lionel.

Among the public mourners at his funeral were many from the golfing fraternity; among those from cricket were FS Jackson (MCC representative), JL Daniell (Somerset) and AG Barrett and AE Newton, the Somerset president and old county wicket-keeper. It was also stated that two people were refused entry to the funeral, though it does not state why. Although he died at a relatively young age, he outlived many of the team that took Somerset into the Championship in 1891. These included George Nichols, Ted Tyler, Sam Woods, Herbie Hewett, Gerald Fowler and Vernon Hill.

In his will he left an estate valued at £16,654 (in 2016 money, £980,000). He left £5,000 to his son Henry. His daughter Mollie was not mentioned, which seems odd, but his granddaughter Daphne Felicity Birbeck was left most of his shares. His house 'Dodhill' was sold by auction in early August. The house was clearly a fair size as it had three reception rooms, six bedrooms and an office. There was also a large garden which included a vegetable area, a small orchard, an outbuilding and a garage, so for a man on his own, it was a very large property. It is not known how much it eventually fetched. All his antiques, furniture and other household items were sold over the next 12 months at various auctions; quite sad for his life to be dismantled in such a manner.

In the months after his death, a number of articles cropped up in a various newspapers across Britain, most commenting on his style as a batsman but also his work, and membership of many committees that he served on over the years. His obituary in the 1934 Wisden Almanack praised his batting style and mentioned some of his main batting feats; what is surprising is that it did not mention his golfing career as a player or administrator once.

His brother Richard would live to 83 and would die at his home in Budleigh Salterton in Devon in 1955. In his last few years he suffered from poor health. During his life he had been a useful Somerset cricketer, though business limited his appearances like Lionel's. He had been a staff captain during the First World War, signing up when 43, and spending a lot of time in India. Later he became secretary to Surrey County Cricket Club and was joint tour manager on the Bodyline series. Richard was also an air raid warden during the Second World War. He had four children, three boys and a girl; one son, Cyril Palairet went down with his ship HMAS Perth during the Battle of the Java Sea in 1942; his death was reported in a number of newspapers.

Lionel outlived two of his sisters. Evelyn, who was the only sibling to actively play archery like her father (she never won a tournament though) would live to 78, dying in 1950. Lionel's daughter Molly died, aged 65, in London in 1961. His son Henry moved to South Africa and owned a farm; he was known for some eccentric behaviour, and died there aged 64 in 1960. Lionel also had another cousin Ann Palairet who would marry the Earl of Oxford who was a grandson of Herbert Asquith (1852-1928) who had been Prime Minster from 1908 until 1916.

Another cousin was Charles Palairet who was knighted by George VI who was a close friend of his. Charles was a top diplomat and at the outbreak of the Second World War was British Ambassador to Austria; he later served in this capacity in Greece.

Chapter 11
His cricketing legacy

In his career Lionel Palairet scored 15,777 runs at an average of 33.63, hitting 27 centuries in 267 first-class matches. He also played twice for England in 1902. It was for Somerset though that he shone; he held many of the club's batting records for decades.

But who was the man? Little has been written about him other than he was a supreme stylist during the 'golden age' of cricket. The little written about him describes him as being aloof. Lionel had a comfortable upbringing; his father was a top barrister and later judge; Lionel was privately schooled, at Repton then Oxford University; and he was used to having a lot of servants in the house. I think his upbringing in grand surroundings, mixing with only his peers, led him to live as a gentleman. He was ill-prepared to mix with people of lower standing and of a less fortunate background. From this lack of exposure, it would appear that he had trouble communicating and getting the best out of his fellow players on the field, and being approachable off the field.

His brother Richard is reported in some books as being 'rude' and 'abrasive'. In photos Lionel does have an air of authority and the stature of a well-to-do gentleman. The only known film of Lionel was taken as he left the field for lunch in 1901 at Manchester in the Somerset-Lancashire game. He looked the part, being well dressed and wearing his familiar Harlequin cap. He can be seen as a tall, slim figure who walks very grandly whilst chatting to Archie MacLaren. He was also known by the nickname 'Coo' to a number of his fellow players. He also seems fairly reserved and would talk little of his deeds on the cricket field. It was more than once stated that he would talk little of his career and none about his record stand with Hewett, so he seems to have been self-depreciatory about his own ability.

His experience as captain was limited to Repton, his two final years at Oxford and one year at Somerset in 1907. His successes at Oxford were mixed, and for Somerset he had a poor year, though the team was poor. At the end of the season, he attacked his team as lacking spirit and the will to fight. It's possible that he was not a natural captain though at the time most county captains were amateurs; he was struggling with his own form, he seemed unable to act or cope with individual needs of his team, or how he could get the best of them. It did not help that the side changed every game and the batting was at times dire. At worst, the evidence that I have is that he was snobbish and often people of this nature seem aloof to others of a more humble upbringing. Peter Roebuck in his book From *Sammy to Jimmy* stated 'he was a reserved fellow, incapable of inspiring affection save amongst his closest friends'. Not really then in Roebuck's assessment captain material. But it needs to be noted that he was brought up in an upper-class manner, educated well and was a hard worker in his own orbit throughout his life.

He was though well respected in his own circles, joining many committees ranging from cricket to fisheries. He clearly worked hard on these committees, helping as best as he could. It is surprising though that in his obituary in *Wisden* that there is no mention of his connections to golf as he spent almost 25 years of his life as a player and faithful servant to the sport, particularly in Devon where he lived. He won many trophies in his time, played golf for Devon for a number of years and held many top positions, at Devon and English amateur level. Over 50 representatives from the golfing world attended his funeral, yet only a few from cricket, and only one regular former team-mate, the old wicket-keeper AE Newton.

I think this lop-sided attendance is mainly due to the fact that from 1905 he lived most of his life in Devon and golf replaced cricket as his main sport, though he did in 1901 state that hunting was his first love. Lionel too was not a great attender at funerals. The only one I have found him attending was poor Ernest Robson in 1924 who died of cancer, having only retired the year before. Lionel did though send wreaths to many of his old cricket colleagues such as WG Grace, Herbie Hewett and Sam Woods.

Lionel also played county football for Dorset and Somerset, was a good athlete, played hockey and croquet, and enjoyed a game of billiards. He was above all a good loyal worker and a family man; he seems to have put these as his main priorities. He was quite right as he was only an amateur and had to earn a living, which he did well, as he enjoyed a comfortable lifestyle; he liked the nice things in life, he was an early owner of a car and enjoyed bicycle riding.

It was though as a cricketer he will be remembered, as a batsman of class and style. To this end I have managed to look into detail at all his innings, gathering a good picture of him at the wicket, as a bowler, a fielder and even an occasional part time wicket-keeper, and more importantly the legacy he left at Somerset as a fine and great player.

His stance at the wicket was tall, the shots he played seemed to be made with little effort, but with maximum power being achieved. He was mainly a front foot player and was generally noted for being successful only on good wickets, and finding a difficult wicket hard to adjust to. However, there are many instances of him holding an innings together when others could do little, so this statement I think is not quite correct. His most favoured shot seems to have been the drive; he could drive with immense power, and although many innings are littered with comments of 'clean beautiful driving along the turf', there are many others which state 'huge big drives' into the crowd or the outfield. A number of his innings ended with a big drive causing his downfall, often on the boundary. He was good at the drive on either side of the wicket.

Another popular shot was the cut; he did this with power and good placement and often chose the right ball to achieve maximum result. His defence was described as very sound with a flawless technique; above all, his innings were always full of grace and poise and with the minimum of effort.

He also scored his runs at a good pace, often getting after the bowling from the first over. He shared in numerous fast partnerships. He got on well with Sam Woods, his captain for most of his career, as they had little time for draws and slow cricket and they always played positively. Sadly in the Somerset teams the burden was on too few.

It was though for Somerset that he had his best days and set some impressive records that stood for many decades. In his batting career he was dismissed 469 times:

*Previous page, Somerset, 1904: Lionel seated second
from left, next to Sam Woods*

Caught 233 (49 per cent)
Bowled 192 (41pc)
Caught and bowled 18 (4pc)
Leg before wicket 13 (3pc)
Run out 4 (1pc)
Stumped 9 (2pc)

His main mode of dismissal was caught. What is surprising is
that for a front footed player he was only stumped nine times, so
he must have been a good judge of when to advance to spinners.
He was only run out four times, so must have been a good judge of
a run. Sadly his last innings ended in a run out. He was dismissed
most times, 19, by JT Hearne of Middlesex, a right-arm medium
bowler; this was followed by (16) FG Roberts (Gloucestershire)
a left-arm fast bowler. Other regular wicket takers were Johnny
Briggs (14), slow left-arm and Tom Richardson (13), right-arm
fast.

It would appear that Lionel did not have a specific weakness to
a type of bowling, though with the entries of Roberts and Briggs
it is possible he found left-arm a little more testing that the more
conventional right-arm type bowlers. His dominance though was
in matches for Somerset. In 222 appearances he scored 13,851
runs at 35.79; this average was not beaten until Harold Gimblett
who would finish with a slightly better career average of 36.96.

Lionel's 292 against Hampshire, in 1896, remained the county's
highest individual score until Gimblett scored 310 against Sussex
in 1948. Lionel's record of 27 centuries was not beaten until
1948, again by Gimblett, who also overtook Lionel's aggregate
of runs in 1949. Lionel's' Somerset record of carrying his bat
through an innings four times has only been equalled once, by
his colleague Len Braund.

On six occasions Lionel scored a century before lunch, five
of these in 1901; only Viv Richards has managed to equal his
Somerset record. On three occasions he scored over 60 per cent

of the total for a completed innings; only Peter Wight (twice) has achieved this more than once for Somerset. Lionel scored 1,000 runs in a season for Somerset six times, a record until Frank Lee registered his seventh in 1938; it must be noted though that after the First World War, Somerset played considerably more matches. Lionel's record of 1,906 runs in 1901 was not beaten until Frank Lee scored 2,019 in 1938.

On ten occasions Lionel topped the Somerset batting averages; this remains a record. His record of reaching 10,000 runs for Somerset (in 151 matches), was not beaten until Viv Richards achieved this feat in 137 matches in 1982. Lionel's 346 for the first wicket with HT Hewett against Yorkshire in 1892 remains the county record; Lionel also shared in four other 200-plus partnerships for the first wicket. He also added 249 with RCN Palairet against Sussex in 1896 for the second wicket, not beaten until 1923. With CA Bernard he added 262 against Hampshire in 1900; this stand for the third wicket remained the club record until 1960. His presence and weight of runs remains impressive to this day.

As a bowler he generally bowled under-hand lobs, though occasionally he would bowl the odd right-arm off break. He took 143 wickets; he twice took five wickets in an innings, both for Oxford University. His favourite victims were GR Baker (Lancashire) and PF Warner (Middlesex), both four times. He dismissed on three occasions CB Fry, AW Mold, Hylton Phillipson and TC O'Brien. Some other notable scalps included Bobby Abel (twice), TW Hayward, GH Hirst, KS Ranjitsinjhi and AE Stoddart.

As a fielder he took 284 catches and made 14 stumpings. He was generally a deep fielder often at mid-on or long on but on occasions would field in the slips. If Somerset were struggling for a wicket-keeper, he did on occasions keep wicket and generally did a competent job. He caught John Tunnicliffe of Yorkshire six times behind the wicket and Bill Brockwell five times; he also caught WG Grace twice and stumped him; and stumped Ted Wainwright of Yorkshire twice.

As a stylist he left an undiminished mark on the game. HS Altham wrote:

'Of all the great batsman I have been privileged to watch and admire, none has ever given me quite the sense of confident and ecstatic elation as Palairet. A perfect stance, an absolutely orthodox method, power in driving that few have equalled and withal, a classic grace and poise, unruffled even in adversity.'

High praise indeed; I think a fitting way to sum up him up as a player of immense grace and ability. He was pleasant on the eye to all who watched him and left his mark on the game. David Foot states 'he was probably the most stylish batsman to play for the county', a statement that I think Lionel merits.

He had a fine career as a fine graceful batsman but also as a useful lob bowler, good outfielder, and stand-in wicketkeeper who although lost too early to business left a fine record for Somerset. He duly deserves to be remembered as one of the best cricketers to have played for the county; he really was a cricketer 'par excellence'.

*

Appendices

Career statistics

First-class cricket (all in England)
Batting and fielding

Season	Matches	Innings	Not out	Runs	HS	Average	100	50	Caught	St
1890	8	15	0	285	72	19.00	-	2	6	-
1891	18	35	1	821	100	24.14	1	7	12	-
1892	26	46	4	1343	146	31.97	2	7	21	3
1893	19	34	1	871	91	26.39	-	7	26	-
1894	18	34	1	969	181	29.36	2	5	9	-
1895	15	29	1	1313	165	46.89	3	7	14	3
1896	20	35	2	1362	292	41.27	4	4	21	-
1897	12	21	1	593	92	29.65	-	3	14	-
1898	17	29	2	1126	179x	41.70	4	5	15	2
1900	14	27	0	947	161	35.07	1	7	14	-
1901	18	34	1	1906	194	57.75	5	11	16	1
1902	21	38	1	1119	90	30.24	-	5	23	3
1903	11	20	2	637	114	35.38	1	4	9	1
1904	19	34	0	1277	203	37.55	3	5	16	-
1905	3	5	1	126	91	31.50	-	1	1	-
1906	1	2	0	73	42	36.50	-	-	-	-
1907	19	36	0	768	116	21.33	1	2	22	1
1908	6	10	0	231	77	23.10	-	1	8	-
1909	2	4	1	10	6x	3.33	-	-	1	-
Total	267	488	19	5777	292	33.63	27	83	248	14

Bowling

Season	Balls	Maidens	Runs	Wickets	BB	Average	5wI	10wM
1890	743	51	346	12	3-28	28.83	-	-
1891	832	47	382	17	3-13	22.47	-	-
1892	1417	83	724	30	6-84	24.13	2	-
1893	270	16	164	2	1-32	82.00	-	-
1894	399	14	197	6	4-49	32.83	-	-
1895	805	41	490	13	4-32	37.69	-	-
1896	1000	60	536	11	3-50	48.72	-	-
1897	134	5	108	3	2-35	36.00	-	-
1898	471	28	264	3	1-24	88.00	-	-
1900	600	23	329	12	3-46	27.41	-	-
1901	490	13	358	7	3-129	51.14	-	-
1902	480	16	263	12	3-28	21.91	-	-
1903	180	6	100	3	2-28	33.33	-	-
1904	894	28	522	12	3-60	43.50	-	-
1905	84	2	58	0				
1906	12	0	9	0				
Total								
	8811	433	4850	143	6-84	33.91	2	-

Batting and fielding against each opponent

Team	Matches	Inns	Not out	Runs	HS	Average	100	50	Ct	St
Australia (Tests)	2	4	0	49	20	12.25	-	-	2	-
Australians	9	16	1	439	90	29.26	-	-	3	-
Cambridge University	5	10	1	235	98	26.11	-	2	5	-
East of England	1	2	0	58	33	29.00	-	-	-	-
Essex	1	2	0	64	33	32.00	-	-	1	1
Gentlemen of England	4	7	0	227	74	32.42	-	2	2	-
Gentlemen of Philadelphia	2	3	1	51	46x	25.50	-	-	3	-
Gloucestershire	27	49	4	1669	179x	37.08	4	9	33	1
H Philipson's eleven	1	2	0	58	53	29.00	-	1	3	-

Team Matches	Inns	Not out	Runs	HS	Average	100	50	Ct	St
Hampshire									
18	29	3	1372	292	52.76	3	6	12	-
Kent									
25	47	1	1421	116	30.89	1	13	17	4
Lancashire									
31	58	1	1425	182	25.00	2	7	25	-
Marylebone Cricket Club									
8	15	0	350	74	23.33	-	2	4	-
Middlesex									
27	52	2	1623	113x	32.46	3	9	23	-
Nottinghamshire									
4	6	0	207	119	34.50	1	-	6	-
Oxford University									
5	9	0	447	181	49.66	1	2	8	-
Players									
6	12	0	235	54	19.58	-	1	8	-
Players of the South									
1	2	0	39	36	19.50	-	-	-	-
Somerset									
1	2	1	47	43x	47.00	-	-	-	-
South Africans									
3	6	0	137	72	22.83	-	2	6	-
Surrey									
23	42	2	1488	140	37.20	4	6	27	1
Sussex									
27	47	2	1852	194	41.15	2	11	23	-
Warwickshire									
4	6	0	59	22	9.83	-	-	5	-
Worcestershire									
8	15	0	574	203	38.26	1	2	4	3
Yorkshire									
24	45	0	1651	173	36.68	5	5	21	4

Bowling against each opponent

Season	Balls	Maidens	Runs	Wickets	BB	Average	5wI	10wM
Australians	208	8	137	2	1-37	68.50	-	-
Cambridge University	235	13	134	1	1-40	134.00	-	-
East of England	25	3	12	1	1-0	12.00	-	-
Essex	100	7	50	0	-	-	-	-
Gentlemen of England	471	29	267	11	5-98	24.27	1	-
Gentlemen of Philadelphia	38	2	27	0	-	-	-	-
Gloucestershire	587	22	306	13	3-28	23.53	-	-
H Philipson's eleven	209	9	88	4	2-28	22.00	-	-
Hampshire	663	16	458	12	3-46	38.16	-	-
Kent	738	36	407	13	3-50	31.30	-	-
Lancashire	1545	90	751	30	6-84	25.03	1	-
Marylebone Cricket Club	590	33	298	7	2-5	42.57	-	-
Middlesex	622	29	319	14	4-32	22.78	-	-
Nottinghamshire	25	1	12	0	-	-	-	-
Oxford University	359	9	184	8	4-49	23.00	-	-
Players	105	7	62	1	1-26	62.00	-	-
Players of the South	75	2	34	1	1-34	34.00	-	-
Somerset	35	0	30	0	-	-	-	-
South Africans	18	0	8	0	-	-	-	-
Surrey	574	34	298	7	2-50	42.57	-	-
Sussex	1054	58	606	14	3-51	43.28	-	-
Worcestershire	66	3	46	0	-	-	-	-
Yorkshire	469	22	316	4	1-11	79.00	-	-

Sources

Books

ACS First Class Scores 1890-1910

Brown LH, *Victor Trumper and the 1902 Australians*,
   Secker & Warburg, 1981

Cricket A Weekly Record 1890-1909

Foot D, *Sunshine, Sixes and Cider*, David & Charles, 1986

Frith D, *The Golden Age of Cricket 1890-1914*,
   Omega Books, 1983

Green B, *The Wisden Book of Cricketers' Lives*,
   Queen Anne Press, 1986

Jessop GL, *A Cricketer's Log*, Hodder and Stoughton, 1923

Jiggens C, *The Sporting Life of SMJ Woods*,
   Sansom & Company, 1997

John N, *Somerset CCC First Class Records*,
   Limlow Books, 1995

Lawrence E, *Classic Somerset CCC*, Tempus, 2002

Lawrence E, *100 Somerset CCC Greats*, Tempus, 2001

Martin-Jenkins C, *The Wisden Book of County Cricket*,
   Queen Anne Press, 1981

Paine P, *Innings Complete*, Catford Print Centre, 2000

Plumptre G, *The Golden Age of Cricket*,
   Macdonald Queen Anne Press, 1990

Roberts EL, *Cricket in England 1894-1939*, E Arnold & Co, 1946

Roberts R, *Sixty Years of Somerset Cricket*,
   Westway Books, 1952

Roebuck P, *From Sammy to Jimmy*, Partridge Press, 1991

Somerset CCC, *A Photographic History of Somerset CCC
1891-1991*, Barnicotts Ltd, 1991

Webber JR, *The Chronicle of WG*, Limlow Books, 1998

Webber R, *County Cricket Championship*,
Sportsman's Book Club, 1958

Wisden Cricketers' Almanacks 1891-1910

Newspapers

Aberdeen Evening Press; Bath Chronicle and Weekly Gazette;
Belfast News; Bell's Weekly Messenger; Birmingham Daily
Post; Birmingham Mail; Bradford Daily Telegraph; Brighton
Gazette; Bristol Mercury; Derby Mercury; Dundee Courier;

Exeter and Plymouth Gazette; Glasgow Herald; Gloucestershire Chronicle; Kentish Gazette; Lancashire Evening Post, Leeds Intelligencer; London Daily News; The Morning Post: Nottingham Evening Post; Somerset County Gazette; Sporting Life; Taunton Courier; Wells Journal; Western Courier; Yorkshire Evening Post.

Websites

Ancestry; Cricinfo; CricketArchive; The Devon County Golf Union; the British Newspaper Website; Wikipedia.

Other

1891 and 1911 censuses.

Index

Northamptonshire CCC 96
Norton St Philip 18
Nottinghamshire CCC 33, 35-36, 41, 45, 60, 99
Notts County 30

O'Brien, TC 125
OG Radcliffe's X1 15
Old Reptonians (cricket) 14, 95
Oriel College, Oxford 18
Ortega SS 14
Oxford Athletic Club 23
Oxford Cygnets (football) 42
Oxford University (Oxford) 5, 8, 24, 30-31, 37-38, 42-43, 45, 46, 69, 79, 98, 114, 119, 125

Paish, AJ 65
Palairet, Ann (Cousin) 118
Palairet, Caroline Mabel (nee' Laverton) – wife 38,43,47,115,116
Palairet, Charles (uncle) 9,12
Palairet, Charles (cousin) 118
Palairet Cup 104, 106
Palairet, Cyril (nephew) 118
Palairet Rev, CH (uncle) 18
Palairet Edith Veronica (nee Scobell - sister) 9, 116
Palairet, Evelyn Mabel (Molly – daughter) 47, 117-118
Palairet, Evelyn Mary (sister) 9, 118
Palairet, Henry Edward (son) 47, 110, 117-118
Palairet, Henry Hamilton (father) 8, 11, 14, 94, 107
Palairet, John Gwalter (great-great grandfather) 8
Palairet, Laura (Aunt) 117
Palairet, Lionel Charles Hamilton
- Death 116
- General 5, 9, 15, 42, 98, 104, 106-108, 110, 112-114, 120, 124-126

- Golf 97, 104-105, 109, 111, 114, 116
- Repton 12, 13, 16, 21
- Oxford University 16, 18-24, 29-30, 32, 36, 37, 38
- Cricketer 25, 28, 32, 33, 35-36, 39, 41, 43-56, 58-60, 62-63,65-79, 81-82, 86-93, 95, 96, 99-103, 108, 119
- Working (Earl of Devon) 94-95
- England 82-85
- Trip to USA 29
Palairet, Richard Cameron North (brother) 9, 18-19, 22-23, 28, 47, 52, 62, 94, 108, 117, 118, 119, 125
Palairet, Rose Eleanor (sister) 9, 11 (death)
Palairet, Septimus (grandfather) 8
Palairet's, (family) 7, 42
Palmer, AJ 110
Parris, Frederick 53
Paul, Arthur 47
Peel, Robert 35, 37, 72
Philadelphia, County Durham 8
Philadelphians 54, 88
Phillips, Frank 30, 56, 59, 75, 86, 100
Phillips, Jim 16, 55, 67, 72-74
Phillipson, Hylton 125
Pistor, Catherine (married John Gwalter Palairet) 8
Players 32, 35-36, 51, 60
Players of the North 44
Poidevin, Les 91
Porch, RB 54
Portsmouth 116
Portsmouth CC 35, 47, 76, 81
Powderham 107, 111
Poyntz, Massey 99, 102, 107

Quaife, WG 113

Raikes, GB 37
Rampisham, Dorset 12